Online Privacy

Peggy J. Parks

About the Author

Peggy J. Parks holds a bachelor of science degree from Aquinas College in Grand Rapids, Michigan, where she graduated magna cum laude. An author who has written dozens of educational books on a wide variety of topics for young people, Parks lives in Muskegon, Michigan, a town she says inspires her writing because of its location on the shores of beautiful Lake Michigan.

With special thanks to Cherese Cartlidge.

© 2017 ReferencePoint Press, Inc.
Printed in the United States

For more information, contact:
ReferencePoint Press, Inc.
PO Box 27779
San Diego, CA 92198
www.ReferencePointPress.com

ALL RIGHTS RESERVED.
No part of this work covered by the copyright hereon may be reproduced or used in any form or by any means—graphic, electronic, or mechanical, including photocopying, recording, taping, web distribution, or information storage retrieval systems—without the written permission of the publisher.

Picture Credits

Cover: Shutterstock.com/Lightspring
 6: Depositphotos/Mactrunk
10: Depositphotos/2nix
13: Depositphotos/seewhatmitchsee
16: Ariel Skelley Blend Images/Newscom
22: David Becker/Stringer/Getty Images
27: Depositphotos/ajafoto
31: Klaus Guldbrandsen/Science Source
35: Depositphotos/tulpahn
38: Associated Press
41: Depositphotos/Thomaspajot
47: Depositphotos/londondeposit
50: Depositphotos/gpointstudio
53: Handout/Getty Images
59: Shutterstock.com/Frederic Legrand
63: Mark Wilson/Getty Images

LIBRARY OF CONGRESS CATALOGING-IN-PUBLICATION DATA

Names: Parks, Peggy J.,- author.
Title: Online Privacy / by Peggy J. Parks.
Description: San Diego, CA : ReferencePoint Press, Inc., 2017. | Series:
  Digital issues series | Includes bibliographical references and index. | Audience: Grade 9 to 12.
Identifiers: ISBN 9781601529886 (hardback) | ISBN 9781601529893 (eBook)
Subjects: LCSH: Computer privacy--Juvenile literature. | Computer crimes--Prevention--
  Juvenile literature.

CONTENTS

Introduction — 4
A Slow, Steady Loss

Chapter One — 8
The Digital Trail

Chapter Two — 20
Privacy and the Internet of Things

Chapter Three — 32
Privacy, Security, and Social Media

Chapter Four — 44
The Perils of Diminishing Online Privacy

Chapter Five — 56
Protecting Online Privacy

Source Notes — 67

Organizations to Contact — 72

For Further Research — 75

Index — 77

INTRODUCTION

A Slow, Steady Loss

On June 1, 2015, via live videoconference, Timothy D. Cook spoke at an event sponsored by the Electronic Privacy Information Center. Cook, who is Apple's chief executive officer (CEO), stressed that people should not have to choose between their online activities and privacy. "People have a fundamental right to privacy," he said. "The American people demand it, the Constitution demands it, morality demands it."[1]

In particular, Cook had harsh words for companies that benefit monetarily from collecting, storing, and sharing customers' personal information. "They're gobbling up everything they can learn about you and trying to monetize it," he said. Although Cook did not call out any companies by name, he clearly was referring to the Silicon Valley giants Facebook, Google, Yahoo!, Twitter, and others whose business models revolve around collecting and sharing customer data. "Some of the most prominent and successful companies have built their businesses by lulling their customers into complacency about their personal information," Cook said. "We think that's wrong."[2]

The Real Cost of "Free"

Cook's reference to companies "gobbling up" customers' personal data was a colloquial term for a practice known as data mining. In exchange for not having to pay to use social media (like Facebook or Twitter), portal sites/search engines (like Google or Yahoo!), or other free apps and online platforms, people consent to have their personal information collected. The amount and type of information varies, depending on what Internet users reveal about themselves and what device they use. It may include personal data such as their birth date, hometown, current residence, education, job history, political affiliation, and religious views. It may be which numbers they frequently call or text, their purchasing habits and preferences, which medications they order online, and personal and revealing details about friends and family.

While doing research for his book *Terms of Service*, author Jacob Silverman was troubled to learn how extensive Facebook's data collection practices are. Not only does the company track everything users do on the site, including what they post, whose profiles they look at, how often they log on, and where they log in from; Facebook also tracks statements that users write into the status bar and then delete. "I think that's revealing of Facebook's mind-set," says Silverman, "which is that they really want to know everything we're . . . doing and thinking and our responses to pretty much almost any form of stimuli. And I think that's really troubling and not really a fair arrangement."[3]

Although collecting users' personal data has been a standard practice for years, privacy advocates and security experts warn it is getting out of control. Cook feels strongly about that, and he stresses that customers should never have to forfeit their right to online privacy for a service they "think is free but actually comes at a very high cost." This is especially true, he says, as people increasingly store sensitive data about their health, their finances, their jobs, their relationships, and other aspects of their lives on smartphones, laptops, and other devices. In his speech Cook emphasized that customers should be in control of their own personal information and not be unconcerned about losing their privacy. "You might like these so-called free services," he said, "but we don't think they're worth having your email, your search history and . . . even your family photos data mined and sold off for god knows what advertising purpose."[4]

> "People have a fundamental right to privacy. The American people demand it, the Constitution demands it, morality demands it."[1]
>
> —Timothy D. Cook, chief executive officer of Apple.

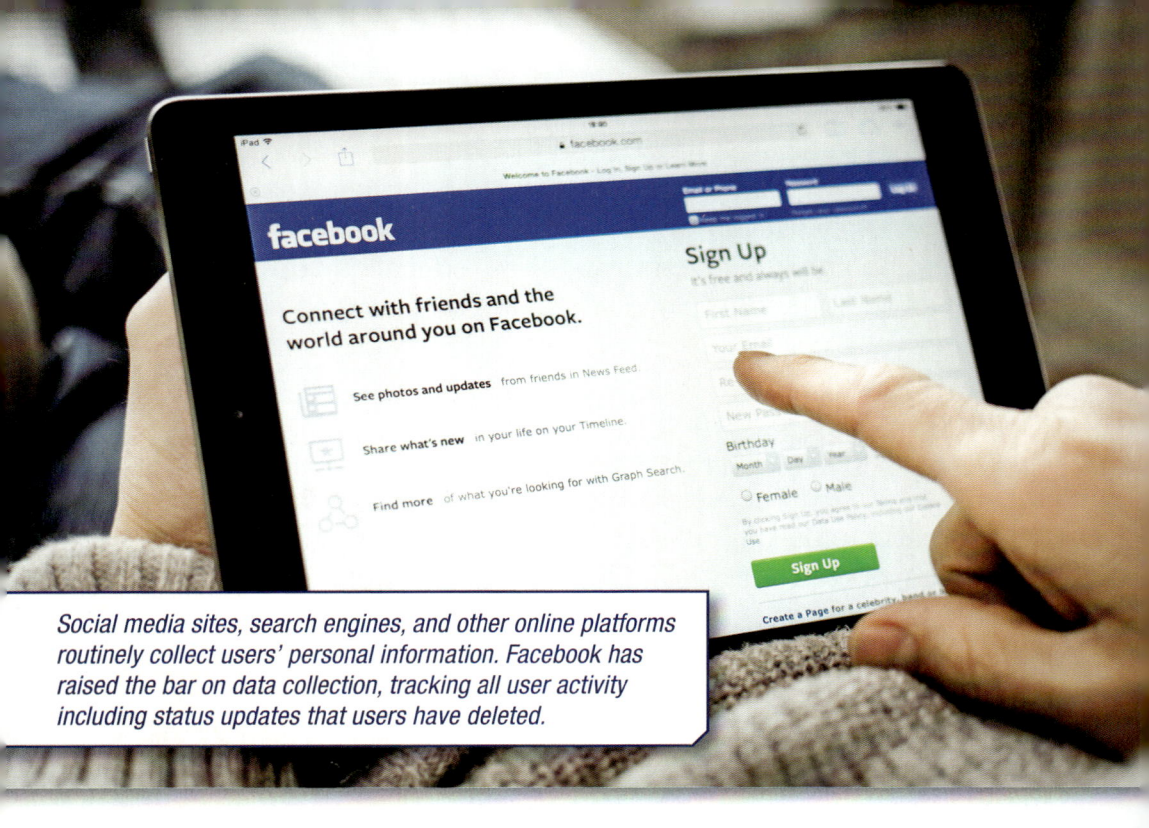

Social media sites, search engines, and other online platforms routinely collect users' personal information. Facebook has raised the bar on data collection, tracking all user activity including status updates that users have deleted.

Acceptance, Not Approval

When marketers are challenged about data mining practices, their rationale has typically been that customers think exchanging their personal data for discounts or other perks is a fair trade. "People are always willing to trade privacy and information when they see the direct value of sharing that information,"[5] says Mike Zaneis, chief counsel for the Interactive Advertising Bureau in Washington, DC. But according to a 2015 study, consumers are not quite as enthusiastic about it as Zaneis claims. In fact, the study found that people *do* care about the loss of their privacy, but they feel powerless to do anything about it.

The study was led by Joseph Turow, a professor at the Annenberg School for Communication at the University of Pennsylvania. More than fifteen hundred adult Internet users participated by responding to statements about online privacy. When asked if it was fair for companies to offer discounts without explaining that personal information would be collected, 91 percent said it was not. Nearly 85 percent said they wanted to have control over what marketers could learn about them online, but most had come to accept that they had little control over it. "Americans believe it is futile to manage what companies can learn about them," Turow and his coauthors explain. "Our study reveals that more than half do not want to lose control over their information but also believe this loss of control has already happened."[6] With most every question on the survey, participants dispelled the myth that they were happy to give away their personal information in exchange for benefits.

Marketers' current practice of collecting and compiling customers' personal data is rife with potential problems that researchers are only beginning to study. One of the best known—and potentially devastating—of these problems is the risk of a major data breach. Consumers have no idea how and where their personal data is stored, and they are helpless to stop malicious vandals from stealing it. During 2015 there were hundreds of data breaches that targeted businesses, government agencies, and other institutions and exposed more than 100 million consumer records. When such a breach happens, the risk to consumers can range from humiliation and embarrassment (if they are discovered doing something they should not be doing) to identity theft and criminal victimization.

> "Americans believe it is futile to manage what companies can learn about them."[6]
>
> —Joseph Turow, Michael Hennessy, and Nora Draper, researchers at the University of Pennsylvania's Annenberg School for Communication.

Although some loss of privacy is inevitable and expected—an inherent by-product of participating in the digital world—people should not assume that they are powerless. In fact, security and privacy experts warn people not to become resigned to the loss of their personal data. Internet users should become educated about why certain data is being collected and what is happening with it, and they must speak up when they have concerns. If they do nothing, they are forfeiting their rights and their privacy will likely erode even more than it already has. "People are starting to be so frustrated about privacy that they believe they can't get anything better," says Rainey Reitman of the Electronic Frontier Foundation. "We have to push back against that idea."[7]

CHAPTER ONE

The Digital Trail

After several years of covering online privacy issues for the *Wall Street Journal*, investigative journalist Julia Angwin wrote a book called *Dragnet Nation*. As part of her research, Angwin tracked down her own digital trail, meaning all the bits and pieces of personal data that had accumulated online. This took a year and proved to be a daunting, often discouraging task. "There's a lot of data out there about all of us," says Angwin. "I tried to find my trail and I was shocked at how vast it was." Particularly disturbing was the magnitude of Angwin's personal data that had been collected and stored over the years. "I found all my web searches stored on Google servers dating back to 2006," she says. "Everyone I'd ever friended or declined their friend request on Facebook—all of it was stored in all these different servers. And that was just the tip of the iceberg."[8]

During her yearlong quest, Angwin spent hundreds of hours scouring the Internet in an attempt to track down her personal data. She also bought expensive tech gadgets to make herself as anonymous as possible while online. Finally, she became so frustrated she gave up, deciding that trying to be anonymous online was an insurmountable task. "After spending a year doing this, I felt this is not something any normal person would do or should do,"[9] she says. From her experience, Angwin learned how difficult it is for people to control the spread of their own data once it is out there. Their only option is to give up using a cell phone or any other Internet-connected device, but few people, Angwin included, are willing to take such extreme precautions to protect their online privacy.

"Digital Bread Crumbs"

The reason tracking down and controlling one's data can seem impossible is because so much of it exists in so many different places. Virtually every time people use the Internet, no matter what they are using it for, they leave behind clues about themselves and what they were doing. "As we shop online, as we browse the Web, whenever we post to a social network, we will be leaving digital bread crumbs,"[10] says Edith Ramirez, chairwoman of the Federal Trade Commission (FTC). This information is collected and used for various purposes, such as tailoring online advertising to customers based on their known preferences.

People may find such information gathering to be intrusive and a breach of privacy, or not mind this level of customization. No matter their perspective, however, the practice has been going on for years; the only thing new is that data is now collected digitally. In an effort to grow their businesses and improve service, companies have always tried to better understand their customers and potential customers. Pre-Internet companies conducted telephone surveys and offered discounts in newspaper ads, recording information about people who redeemed the ads. Customers filled out information cards in exchange for being added to mailing lists that would notify them of special offers and events. Much like today's data mining, these and other marketing techniques offered customers some kind of benefit in exchange for their personal information. The Internet, however, has vastly expanded companies' ability to collect and store customer data—and whether that is good or bad is largely a matter of opinion.

> "There's a lot of data out there about all of us. I tried to find my trail and I was shocked at how vast it was."[8]
>
> —Julia Angwin, an investigative journalist and author of the book *Dragnet Nation*.

Online Identifiers

There are a number of ways people leave digital tracks, with cookies among the most common. Cookies are tiny packets of unique identity data that are deposited on a device after someone has been online. These data may include an e-mail address; Internet protocol (IP) address (which identifies the device that was used to get on the Internet); what the user searched for or bought online; and/or other identifying factors. "Cookies are great," says Mark Stockley, founder of the web consultancy firm Compound Eye. "They're used by websites to keep track of you between accesses—not just between visits from day to day, but between individual web page requests after you've logged in. Without cookies, we couldn't have things like login sessions, so there would be no Twitter, no eBay and no online banking."[11]

Other functions performed by cookies are not necessarily for the benefit of users. Referring to cookies as "virtual spies," the computer software company Panda Security explains that these data packets can monitor users' online activity, including pages they visit most often and topics that interest them. "If, say, an ad for a food product appears on your screen after you visit a restaurant page, don't be too surprised. Thanks to cookies, advertising can

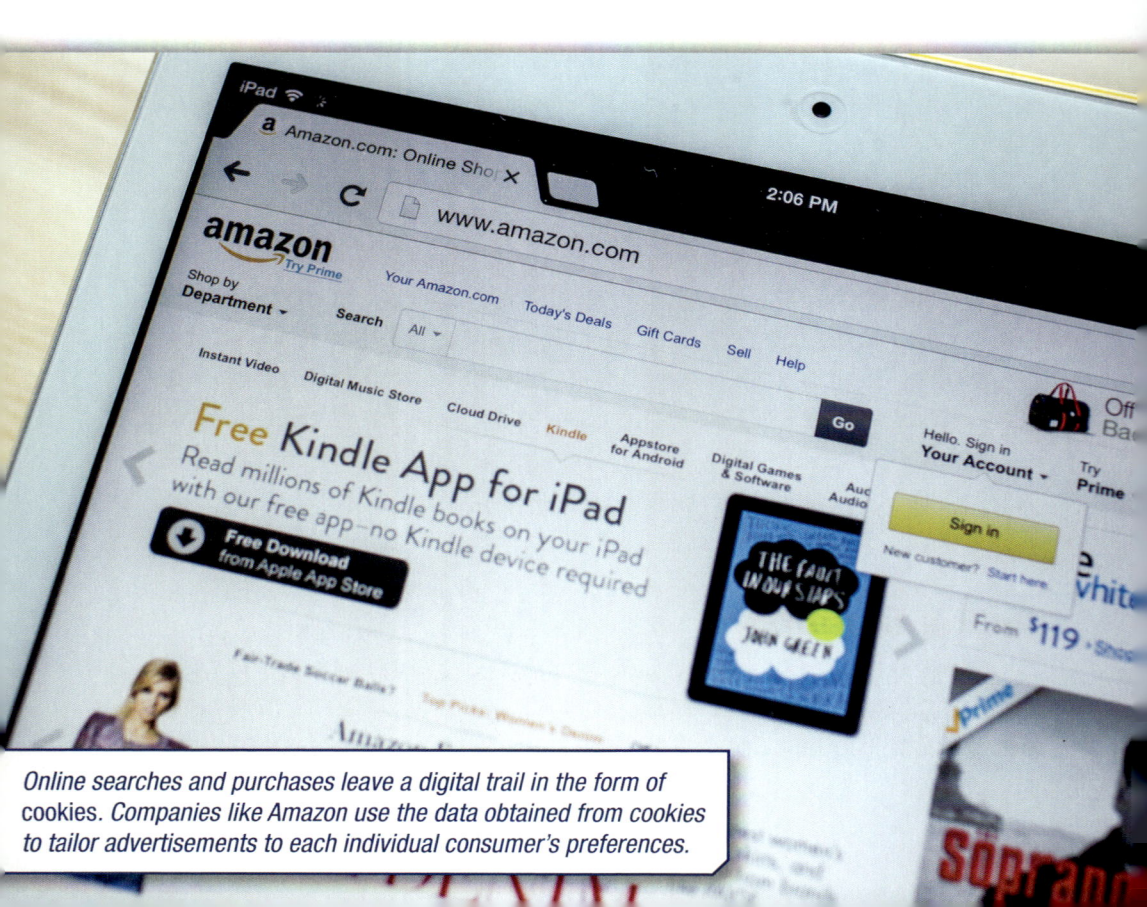

Online searches and purchases leave a digital trail in the form of cookies. Companies like Amazon use the data obtained from cookies to tailor advertisements to each individual consumer's preferences.

be tailored to consumers' preferences," says Panda Security. The company goes on to explain that even though cookies are usually safe and do not pose threats to users, "it is not always clear in whose hands the collected data ends up or where it is stored."[12]

Another source of digital tracking is exchangeable image file (EXIF) data, which digital cameras (including phone cameras) capture whenever a picture is taken. EXIF data contain information about the photo such as the time and date, what camera was used to take it, shutter speed, and other unique details. This is a benefit for photographers because EXIF information helps identify and organize photos. But the data can also create privacy issues because it includes geolocation information, meaning the exact place where the photo was snapped. "Do you see the potential problem?" says technology trainer Timothy L. Warner. "This means that if I share a cute digital picture of my cat with my friend, and my friend posts the picture to her Facebook wall, lots of people could (in theory) view the exact location of my home, which is probably where I took the cute picture in the first place."[13]

> "Without cookies, we couldn't have things like login sessions, so there would be no Twitter, no eBay and no online banking."[11]
>
> —Mark Stockley, founder of the web consultancy firm Compound Eye.

As intrusive as geolocation can be, it can also lead to positive outcomes. In 2012 EXIF data pinpointed the exact whereabouts of three Burger King employees in Mayfield Heights, Ohio, who had committed a malicious act. It involved a photo of a man from the knees down who (wearing shoes) was standing in tubs of lettuce. The photo was posted to the image-based social media site 4chan with the caption, "This is the lettuce you eat at Burger King."[14] Although it was posted anonymously, other 4chan users were angry about the photo and tracked it down using EXIF data. They identified the Burger King where it was taken and contacted the local newspaper *Cleveland Scene*, which in turn notified Burger King management. The three employees were identified and immediately fired.

Supercookies and Digital Fingerprints

Of the various tactics companies use to track customer data, one that is especially troubling to security and privacy experts is the supercookie. Also called permacookies and zombie cookies, these online trackers allow data to be re-created after users delete the more traditional cookies. Thus, supercookies are designed to be permanently stored on a user's computer—which means they stubbornly resist all efforts to remove them. Normal procedures for deleting cookies will not get rid of supercookies, nor will clearing the cache, erasing browser history, or running antispyware or adware removal programs.

Eugene Kuznetsov, cofounder of the Boston, Massachusetts, online privacy company Abine, refers to supercookies as the next wave of intrusive digital tracking devices. "What we have here is a privacy arms race," he says. "This desire to track Internet users is like a parasite. Anything you put in a browser is constantly being examined by websites and advertisers to implement more tracking."[15] Kuznetsov and other privacy experts say that supercookies make it more difficult than ever for people to stay anonymous while online.

A tracking technique known as digital fingerprinting is even more challenging for users to control than supercookies. Fingerprints track users based on the unique characteristics of their devices, such as web browser configuration (add-ons and fonts installed), the browser's version information, and even its clock setting. Unlike cookies and supercookies, digital fingerprints leave *no* evidence on a computer, as the Privacy Rights Clearinghouse explains: "Unfortunately, fingerprinting is generally invisible, difficult to prevent, and semi-permanent. There's no easy way to delete fingerprints that have been collected." A particular kind of fingerprinting, known as canvas fingerprinting, works by instructing a user's browser to draw a hidden image. "Because each computer

> "This desire to track Internet users is like a parasite. Anything you put in a browser is constantly being examined by websites and advertisers to implement more tracking."[15]
>
> —Eugene Kuznetsov, cofounder of the Boston, Massachusetts, online privacy company Abine.

draws the image slightly differently," says the Privacy Rights Clearinghouse, "these images can be used to assign a number that uniquely identifies your device."[16] According to the investigative news group ProPublica, 5 percent of the top one hundred thousand websites use canvas fingerprinting to track users' data.

The Data Trade

All the pieces of online information that are collected—an inconceivable quantity of it—are gathered on a regular basis by Google, Facebook, Yahoo!, Twitter, and other such companies. But another important player in the collecting and selling of customer data—one that few people know about—is the data broker. Also known as information brokers, the sole reason these firms are in business is to collect, organize, and sell personal data to companies that seek information about people. According to Ramirez, data brokers "collect massive amounts of information about all of us. And what is astonishing is the sheer breadth of their data collection and data practices."[17]

Social media posts and tweets are a rich source of personal user information for data brokers. These brokers collect, organize, and sell personal data to companies seeking information about consumer behavior and interests.

The information collected by data brokers can be taken from a wide variety of sources, including social media posts and tweets, Google searches, purchases from Internet sellers, online job applications, criminal records, medical records, and warranty card registration information. Buyers of this data may include marketing firms, government agencies, insurance companies, financial institutions, and other data brokers. "Who knows where [our data] might end up?" says journalist and author Jacob Silverman. "Governments, corporate marketing departments, research scientists, prospective employers, advertising firms, insurers—practically anyone interested in large amounts of consumer data has reason to make deals with these companies."[18]

The exact number of data brokers is unknown, although the World Privacy Forum estimates there are about four thousand of them. "No one even knows how many companies there are trafficking our data," says cybersecurity expert Julie Brill. "But it's certainly in the thousands." Brill adds that as data brokers accumulate information about people, it is filed into digital profiles. "I think most people have no idea that it's being collected and sold," she says, "and that it is personally identifiable about them, and that the information is basically a profile of them."[19] Even though much remains unknown about data brokers, the FTC is aware of many of them. One of the largest is Acxiom, a data brokerage company located in Little Rock, Arkansas. Acxiom has approximately eight thousand clients and collects personal information on an estimated 700 million consumers worldwide. Other major players in the data brokerage field include Corelogic, BlueKai, Datalogix, Epsilon, eBureau, and PeekYou.

Digital Dossiers

The FTC, along with other government agencies and privacy advocates, has been closely watching the data brokerage industry for a number of years. Tim Sparapani, a former privacy lawyer for the American Civil Liberties Union (ACLU) and director of public policy for Facebook, says that most people have no idea how much of their personal information is being collected and sold. He

Apps and Privacy

According to the Pew Research Center, nearly 90 percent of American adults aged eighteen to forty-nine and 70 percent of teens have a smartphone. Those who have smartphones typically download a number of mobile applications, more commonly known as apps. When people install an app, they allow it to access certain data on their smartphone; a messaging app, for instance, needs permission to access the user's contact list, as well as Wi-Fi. But some apps ask for access that they really do not need, such as a flashlight app requesting access to a user's location or contacts.

Gary Kovacs, an Internet privacy expert and technology company CEO, had an interesting experience when his daughter asked him to download a children's game for her phone in 2015. The user agreement was long and illegible on a mobile phone. Upon closer inspection, Kovacs realized the agreement said: "We and third-party service providers collect such information from you through your mobile device, including your name, user name, profile pictures, telephone number, device identifiers, email address, contacts, GPS location, browser history, chat or messaging activity." Because of the vast intrusion the game would have into his daughter's privacy, Kovacs did not download it. He says that consumers need to become more aware of such privacy violations instead of accepting them without question.

Gary Kovacs, "Why Online Privacy Matters," World Economic Forum, August 7, 2015. www.weforum.org.

adds that people would be stunned to learn how they are being categorized based on factors such as age, income, political leanings, and religious affiliations. People are also profiled according to their medical history, as Sparapani explains: "You can buy from any number of data brokers, by malady, the lists of individuals in America who are afflicted with a particular disease or condition."[20]

These maladies include everything from alcoholism and clinical depression to cancer, heart disease, and rare genetic disorders.

According to Adam Tanner, a fellow at the Institute for Quantitative Social Science at Harvard University, a growing number of data brokerage firms specialize in gathering medical information. This includes hundreds of millions of patient records from hospitals and doctor's offices, as well as records from prescription medications, insurance claims, and laboratory tests. Tanner says that by law, people's identities are supposed to be kept secret. The companies that sell medical information to data brokers strip the records of names, Social Security numbers, and detailed addresses to protect people's privacy. However, Tanner says it is possible for a person's identity to be revealed, which can lead to serious privacy problems for patients. "The entire health care system depends on patients trusting that their information will be kept confidential," he says. "When they learn that others have in-

A pharmacist discusses a new prescription with a customer. Some data brokers specialize in gathering medical information including records of a patient's prescription medications, medical procedures, and insurance claims.

sights into what happens between them and their medical providers, they may be less forthcoming in describing their conditions or in seeking help."[21]

Aside from medical history, people's digital profiles (often called dossiers) are categorized in specific and often derogatory ways. "The amount of detail contained in these consumer 'dossiers' is astonishing," says the application development firm Sherbit. For example, a data broker called Paramount Lists sells the names of people with alcohol or gambling addictions, and Response Solutions sells lists of people who suffer from bipolar disorder. A data brokerage firm called Statlistics, says Sherbit, "has lists of 'gay and lesbian adults,' possibly by making inferences from bars or clubs where they've used a credit card. InfoUSA can tell you who is a 'suffering senior,' or a 'gullible' one."[22]

A May 2014 report by the FTC states that data brokers often segment people of lower incomes in minority communities, titling their digital dossiers "Urban Scramble" and "Mobile Mixers," both of which refer to Hispanic and African American consumers with low incomes. Older low-income consumers may be placed in the "Rural Everlasting" category, which comprises men and women over age sixty-six with low educational attainment and low net worth. Other segments focus on consumers' interests, such as "Truckin' & Stylin'" and "Health & Wellness Interest." "While some of these segments seem innocuous," say the authors of the FTC report, "others rely on characteristics, such as ethnicity, income level, and education level, which seem more sensitive and may be disconcerting."[23]

Shadowy Entities

The field of data mining is murky and mysterious, with far more unknown about data brokerage firms than is known. According to Sparapani, these companies have been "flying under the radar for years, preferring that people know as little as possible about the industry and the information that's being collected and sold."[24] Users' data exists online, and can be tracked down if people know how to go about doing so. But as Julia Angwin found out,

Little-Known Partnerships

Most consumers are not aware that many companies they do business with sell their personal data to data brokers. These firms categorize the information into segments (such as low-income elderly people or parents who may be in the market for a new vehicle) and store it in massive databases. When companies contact data brokers to ask for a particular segment, the brokers trawl their databases for the e-mail addresses of individuals that fit that description. The brokers use a special process to anonymize the information, which is then forwarded to the buyer.

One example of this is a partnership between Facebook and the major data brokerage firm Acxiom. When Facebook receives the anonymized data from Acxiom, it matches the data to Facebook user profiles and then displays targeted ads to the individuals who fit into the particular categories. "To serve advertisements," says the application development firm Sherbit, "Facebook creates 'Partner Categories,' 'targeting clusters' that combine information collected by the social network (your posts, photos, geo-location data, etc.) with the data brokers' record of 'off-Facebook activity,'" meaning transactions that occur outside of Facebook. Sherbit adds that Facebook users likely have no idea that whenever they use a credit card for purchases, that information is shared with Facebook. "Facebook could hypothetically serve soda ads to teenagers who recently purchased a soft drink at a convenience store," says Sherbit, "or diaper ads to parents who bought baby food at a department store."

Sherbit, "Facebook Partners with Shadowy 'Data Brokers' to Farm Your Information," April 16, 2015. www.sherbit.io.

---

it is extremely difficult to wade through someone's digital trail to find their personal data. Also like her, many give up after finding the task complicated and seemingly impossible.

In August 2015 the FTC filed formal complaints against two data brokerage companies that had illegally sold sensitive financial information of at least five hundred thousand people. The companies, Sequoia One LLC and Gen X Marketing Group, collected financial information about people who had sought payday loans. The data brokers sold the information to third parties, including Florida-based Ideal Financial Solutions. The latter then illegally accessed the consumers' bank accounts and stole more than $7 million. "Companies that collect people's sensitive information and give it to scammers can expect to hear from the FTC," says Jessica Rich, director of the FTC's Bureau of Consumer Protection. She adds that cases like this offer a warning about the loss of online privacy. "If you can buy information so freely, sensitive information, and use it for fraud, it shows that the availability of detailed consumer data can harm them in very tangible ways."[25]

> "Companies that collect people's sensitive information and give it to scammers can expect to hear from the FTC."[25]
>
> —Jessica Rich, director of the FTC's Bureau of Consumer Protection.

The Digital Dilemma

Technology has changed people's lives in numerous ways, affording them new ways to conduct business, communicate with friends, watch the news, and be entertained. But the inevitable result of people's growing online presence is that their privacy is shrinking. Their digital trail is being captured, categorized, and sold to companies that may use it for targeted advertising or for other purposes that range from questionable to dishonest.

CHAPTER TWO

Privacy and the Internet of Things

In a June 2015 essay, Keith Winstein described his involvement in an intriguing project during the late 1990s: being one of the first people to connect a Coca-Cola machine to the Internet. "We thought it was pretty awesome," he says, "that you could, in theory, make the machine dispense a Coke from your desktop computer without having to walk over to it."[26] Winstein, now a computer science professor at Stanford University, adds that everyone in his field knew it was only a matter of time before more items would be connected to the Internet—and they were correct.

Today, in addition to electronic devices, a fast-growing number of household appliances and other products are online, forming what is known as the Internet of Things. "Fridges, smoke detectors, thermostats, furnaces, cars, light bulbs and toasters are all being networked," says Winstein. "The benefits of all this connectivity will probably be greater than our Internet Coke machine." Despite the potential benefits, however, Winstein offers a chilling prophecy of what lies ahead: "There's also a pretty good argument that the Internet of Things is going to be a security and privacy disaster."[27]

The Vulnerability of Things

One of the biggest security risks associated with the Internet of Things comes from malicious vandals who hack into networks or individual products. "It is a software truism," says Winstein, "that anything connected to the Internet needs to be patched regularly," meaning updated with fixes for known security issues. That works fine for desktop or laptop computers because manufacturers continuously provide patches. But according to Winstein, the same will not be true for all the products that will eventually be online. "Inevitably," he warns, "bad guys will have their way with them."[28]

This sort of malicious hacking is occurring today. According to an investigation by the security firm Proofpoint, hackers launched a cyberattack on tens of thousands of "smart" home appliances between December 23, 2013, and January 6, 2014. The appliances, including refrigerators, televisions, and other products, were hooked up to insecure Internet networks. The hackers used the appliances to send out 750,000 malicious spam e-mails, typically sent in bursts of 100,000 three times per day. "The 'Internet of Things' holds great promise for enabling control of all of the gadgets that we use on a daily basis," says Michael Osterman, principal analyst at Osterman Research. "It also holds great promise for cybercriminals who can use our homes' routers, televisions, refrigerators and other Internet-connected devices to launch large and distributed attacks."[29]

> "The 'Internet of Things' . . . holds great promise for cybercriminals who can use our homes' routers, televisions, refrigerators and other Internet-connected devices to launch large and distributed attacks."[29]
>
> —Michael Osterman, principal analyst at Osterman Research.

Patrick Ziselberger, an information technology (IT) manager from Vermont, also believes that the Internet of Things presents enormous security issues. This is largely because there is no mechanism for security patches to be installed on the vast array of *things* connected to the Internet. "So, over time," says Ziselberger, "your 'smart TV' can get code inserted by malicious parties." Also, he says, some features on smart TVs present serious privacy issues. Among such features are the "learning algorithms" used by Samsung on televisions with voice commands and on Microsoft's Xbox One. "They leave the mic on all the time," says

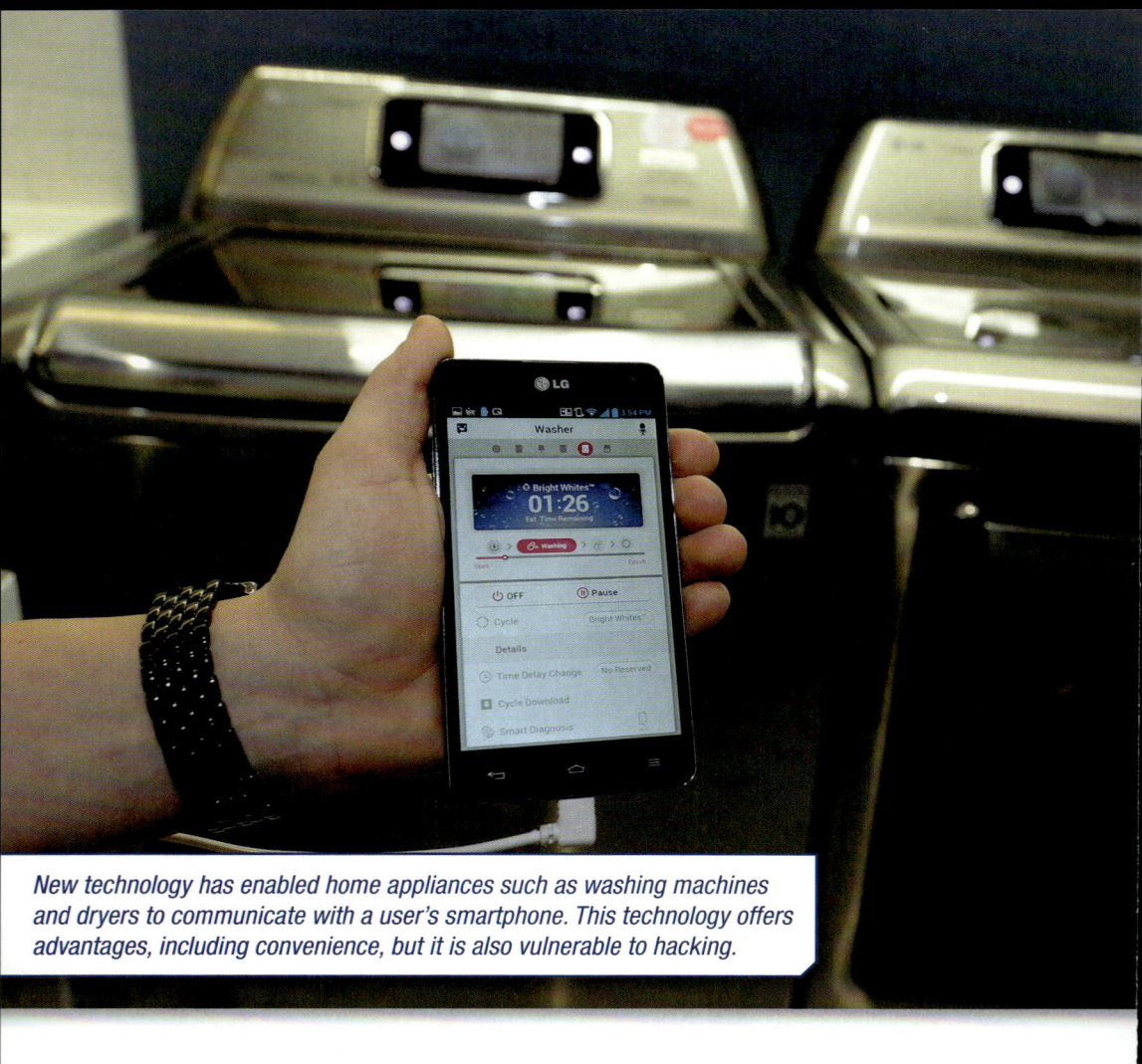

New technology has enabled home appliances such as washing machines and dryers to communicate with a user's smartphone. This technology offers advantages, including convenience, but it is also vulnerable to hacking.

Ziselberger, "record what's going on in the room, and send it back to corporate headquarters. This is ostensibly to improve voice recognition—but really, do you want Microsoft listening in on all of your conversations?"[30]

An additional concern is that all of these interconnected devices share information among themselves about their users. That means if someone hacks into one device, it would result in a domino effect—the hacker would have access to all information on all devices the owner has used. "The cybersecurity challenges are particularly vexing, as the Internet of Things increases the opportunities for attack and amplifies the consequences of any breach,"[31] says James Manyika, a director of the business and economic firm McKinsey Global Institute.

22

Vulnerable Smart Cars—and Drivers

One pressing concern about the Internet of Things is the vulnerability of smart vehicles; specifically, vehicles that have computerized online functions. The computers in smart cars, known as electronic control units (ECUs), are becoming more and more common on modern vehicles. A March 2016 joint bulletin from the FBI, US Department of Transportation, and the National Highway Traffic Safety Administration (NHTSA) describes the many functions ECUs perform: "These ECUs control numerous vehicle functions from steering, braking, and acceleration, to the lights and windshield wipers. A wide range of vehicle components also have wireless capability: from keyless entry, ignition control, and tire pressure monitoring, to diagnostic, navigation, and entertainment systems."[32]

Because vehicles have so many computerized functions, they are becoming increasingly vulnerable to hacking by malicious individuals who could unlock doors, disable a vehicle's heating and cooling system, and even render brakes and other critical functions useless. Another potentially dangerous scenario might involve a thief who steals a couple's car while they are out to dinner. The thief could have the computer's GPS guide the car to the couple's house. Then, using the garage door opener many people keep inside their car, the thief could gain entry to the garage and even the house, robbing it with the secure knowledge that the couple is out for the night.

These and other potential risks have motivated several auto manufacturers to implement safety measures to make vehicles more secure against hacking. For example, in 2015 BMW AG announced it had addressed a security flaw in its vehicles that could have allowed hackers to remotely unlock the doors of up to 2.2 million cars. Also in 2015, General Motors (GM) became aware of a vulnerability in its 2013 Chevrolet Volt, in which hackers could potentially take over functions such as opening doors and starting engines. GM learned about the vulnerability from Samy Kamkar, a hacker who runs the YouTube channel Applied Hacking. Based on information from Kamkar, GM promptly addressed the vulnerability and issued a security update.

Snoopy Self-Driving Cars

In a 2016 *Atlantic* article, Adrienne LaFrance writes about the driverless cars of the future and their inevitable role in eroding privacy. LaFrance's hypothetical scenario opens with a car owner stepping into a driverless car and seeing a destination appear on a screen. A humanoid voice says, "Good morning" and calls the owner by name. The owner requests coffee, and the voice responds, "Peet's coffee, half-a-mile away." The car then recommends picking up the dry cleaning, having lunch at a favorite vegetarian restaurant, and buying groceries that are on special at the market. Upon arriving at the destination (the owner's office), the car displays the owner's morning schedule, along with a reminder of a colleague's birthday.

As intriguing as this scenario may sound, LaFrance says it has a dark side: the loss of privacy. The car suggested Peet's not because it was the closest coffee place, but because it was a sponsored business. The same was true of the dry cleaner's, which was another sponsored business. The car knew the restaurant was a favorite of the owner's because it had combed through e-mails and used information gained from "listening" to the owner's conversations while riding in the car. Similarly, the car knew which sale items to recommend because it had reviewed past grocery shopping activity. "For self-driving cars to work, technologically speaking, an ocean of data has to flow into a lattice of sophisticated sensors," says LaFrance. She adds that such a futuristic scenario might not become reality for a long time, but "there's no reason to believe it's especially far-fetched."

Adrienne LaFrance, "Self-Driving Cars and the Looming Privacy Apocalypse," *Atlantic*, March 20, 2016. www.theatlantic.com.

These sorts of issues are of particular concern to the NHTSA, FBI, and US Department of Transportation. In the March 2016 joint bulletin, the agencies warned drivers, as well as manufacturers of cars and vehicle components, to beware of potential cybersecurity threats in Internet-connected vehicles. The bulletin cautions that such vehicles are "increasingly vulnerable" to being hacked, and goes on to explain: "While not all hacking incidents may result in a risk to safety—such as an attacker taking control of a vehicle—it is important that consumers take appropriate steps to minimize risk." The agencies are concerned that cybercriminals could potentially take advantage of cars' online software updates and send out fake e-mail messages to owners. If that happened, recipients of the e-mails could be "tricked into clicking links to malicious Web sites or opening attachments containing malicious software."[33]

A Hair-Raising Experiment

Although there have been no reported incidents of hackers actually taking control of a vehicle, hackers without malicious intent have been involved in some realistic experiments. Journalist Andy Greenberg describes one of these in a 2015 *Wired* article. He was driving a Jeep Cherokee, traveling at 70 miles per hour (113 kph), when the vehicle was hacked wirelessly. The hackers, Charlie Miller and Chris Valasek, took control of the Jeep's radio, windshield wipers, air-conditioning, and—most alarmingly—its steering, brakes, and transmission.

To create a simulation that was as realistic as possible, Miller and Valasek did not tell Greenberg what kind of remote attack they would be launching on the Jeep. They merely assured him that they would not do anything life-threatening and said that no matter what happened, he should not panic. Following their instructions, Greenberg drove onto the highway, and soon the hacking commenced. He explains how it unfolded:

> Though I hadn't touched the dashboard, the vents in the Jeep Cherokee started blasting cold air at the maximum setting, chilling the sweat on my back through the in-seat climate control system. Next the radio switched to the local hip hop station and began blaring Skee-lo at full volume. I spun the control knob left and hit the power button, to no avail. Then the windshield wipers turned on, and wiper fluid blurred the glass.[34]

Suddenly, the accelerator stopped working, and Greenberg found himself moving at a crawl on the highway. Cars were getting backed up, and an eighteen-wheeler was bearing down on him from behind. That, he says, is when "the experiment had ceased to be fun." As Miller and Valasek advised, Greenberg did not panic. He did, however, "drop any semblance of bravery, grab my iPhone with a clammy fist, and beg the hackers to make it stop," he says. Later, when he was calmer, Greenberg realized the significance of what he had gone through. He had learned how vulnerable a vehicle can be when under the control of hackers. He says that as manufacturers continue to do everything possible "to turn the modern automobile into a smartphone,"[35] this vulnerability will increase.

> "Our newly talkative devices will keep track of everything we do, and our cars will know everywhere we have been. Privacy will be dead, even within our homes."[36]
>
> —Vivek Wadhwa, a Stanford University scholar and researcher.

Threats to Personal Privacy

As the Internet of Things continues to expand, technology experts warn that this presents a major threat to the security of people's data, and thus to their online privacy. According to Stanford University scholar and researcher Vivek Wadhwa, Google already reads people's personal e-mails and keeps track of what they watch on YouTube in order to deliver targeted advertising to them. "Companies such as Apple and Google want to learn all they can about us so that they can market more products and services to us—and sell our data to others," says Wadhwa. He goes on to say that there is much more to come. "Our newly talkative devices will keep track of everything we do, and our cars will know everywhere we have been. Privacy will be dead, even within our homes."[36]

Wadhwa wonders about the implications of what he sees as the next phase in the ever-growing Internet of Things.

Will we be happy for the manufacturers of our refrigerators to recommend new flavors of ice cream, for our washing machines to suggest a brand of clothing to buy, or for our weight scales to recommend new diet plans? They will have the data necessary for doing this, just as the maker of your smart TV is learning what shows you watch. Will we be happy for criminals and governments to hack our houses and learn even more about who we are and what we think?[37]

This scenario, according to Wadhwa, "is an amazing—and scary—future that we are rapidly heading into."[38]

One of the most serious threats individuals face is the possibility that smart devices in homes will be infiltrated. Malicious vandals could conceivably gain control of a homeowner's lights, heat, and appliances, as well as water pumps, garage doors, smoke detectors, and door locks. "Getting to live the Jetsons' lifestyle has downsides," says technology writer and Fusion editor Kashmir Hill. "As we bring the things in our homes onto the Internet, we run into the same kind of security concerns we have for any connected device: they could get hacked."[39]

The idea that a refrigerator manufacturer might recommend a particular ice-cream flavor to a homeowner sounds far-fetched. Given the advances being made toward interconnectedness, scenarios like this might become common.

Potential Exploitation of Health Data

When privacy and security experts warn about the risks associated with the Internet of Things, this invariably includes people's health and medical data. In 2009, when the American Recovery and Reinvestment Act was signed into law, health care providers were required to switch from paper records to electronic health records (EHRs) no later than 2015. But as the computer systems of health care providers have become increasingly interconnected, this has raised the concern that EHRs are not being properly secured. Wherever that is true, it places tens of thousands of patients' personal information at risk of being exploited by malicious individuals.

In fact, medical data security breaches are already occurring throughout the United States. According to the American Action Forum, breaches of EHRs more than doubled in 2015, at a cost of $50 billion to the health care system. The January 2016 *Bitglass Healthcare Breach Report* reveals that one in three Americans were affected by breaches to their EHRs in 2015—98 percent of which were due to hackers.

> "As we bring the things in our homes onto the Internet, we run into the same kind of security concerns we have for any connected device: they could get hacked."[39]
>
> —Technology writer and Fusion editor Kashmir Hill.

One such breach took place in May 2015 at Medical Informatics Engineering, an Indiana medical software company. The breach was not discovered for nineteen days, and in that time the hackers had access to the medical records of nearly 4 million people. On May 26, 2015, the breach was discovered, and access to the database was shut down. Along with health records, according to the US Department of Health and Human Services, information that was exposed in the breach includes patients' names, birth dates, addresses, and Social Security numbers. "There is a considerable risk of the data being used to commit fraud," says a July 26, 2015, article in the medical publication *HIPAA Journal*. "The data fields exposed would allow a criminal to defraud victims in a number of different ways. Identities could be stolen, false tax returns filed, credit obtained in victims' names and bogus insurance claims could be filed."[40]

Cautionary Words

While some see the Internet of Things as making life streamlined and convenient, others see a huge hassle waiting to happen. One such person is Preston Gralla, contributing editor for *Computerworld* and the author of forty-five books on technology and the Internet. Like many of his peers, he has serious concerns about the Internet of Things. Calling it "our worst personal IT nightmare," Gralla tells of a frustrating experience he had after replacing his Wi-Fi router. He found that his smart TV ("which didn't prove to be particularly smart") as well as his wireless music, laser printer, and other tech gadgets would not work on the new network. After days of trying various tactics, many of which were experimental, Gralla finally had the problems fixed and his gadgets back online and running smoothly. "Now," he says, "imagine this same scenario in the age of the [Internet of Things]."

Gralla goes on to describe the staggering complexity of connecting a household to the Internet of Things. "You replace an old router with a new one. Your refrigerator, oven, microwave, light bulbs, heating system, air conditioner, door locks, security system, and even your toothbrushes (yes, there are already network-connected toothbrushes) were all connected to your old network. Now you need to connect them to your new one." This, says Gralla, will likely be a technical nightmare for the average homeowner. "After all," he says, "if engineers can't even make it easy to connect a printer designed to work on a network, how easy do you think it will be to connect your stove?" Gralla foresees innumerable problems ahead as the Internet of Things continues to grow.

Preston Gralla, "The Internet of Things: Your Worst Nightmare," *Computerworld*, July 7, 2015. www.computerworld.com.

One of the biggest concerns about EHRs is violations of people's privacy. Even when the records have been anonymized (such as when people donate organs or samples to genetic research), data mining software has the ability to reveal the donors' identities. This was shown in 2013 when genetics researcher Yaniv Erlich was able to uncover the identities of fifty anonymous donors to the 1000 Genomes Project. Erlich accomplished this by combining the information posted publicly about the participants, such as their age, with genetic information he found online in a genealogy database.

Erlich, who did not make any of the identities public, was also able to find the names of the participants' entire families, even though the relatives were not part of the project. Amy L. McGuire, a lawyer and ethicist at Baylor College of Medicine in Houston, was among those who were alarmed by the implications of Erlich's revelation. "To have the illusion you can fully protect privacy or make data anonymous is no longer a sustainable position,"[41] says McGuire.

Will the Internet of Things Make Privacy Obsolete?

Because of the rate at which the Internet of Things is growing, its future expansion is inevitable. That means more and more items will be part of it, which will bring about new and challenging privacy and security issues. A January 2015 report by the FTC states that there are more than 26 billion connected devices in use worldwide, "with that number set to rise significantly as consumer goods companies, auto manufacturers, healthcare providers, and other businesses continue to invest in connected devices." The agency acknowledges the positive aspects of this widespread connectivity: "Such devices offer the potential for improved health-monitoring, safer highways, and more efficient home energy use, among other potential benefits." However, the FTC also notes that "connected devices raise numerous privacy and security concerns that could undermine consumer confidence."[42]

> "To have the illusion you can fully protect privacy or make data anonymous is no longer a sustainable position."[41]
>
> —Amy L. McGuire, a lawyer and ethicist at Baylor College of Medicine in Houston.

Justin Brookman of the Center for Democracy & Technology believes that the security challenges inherent in the Internet of

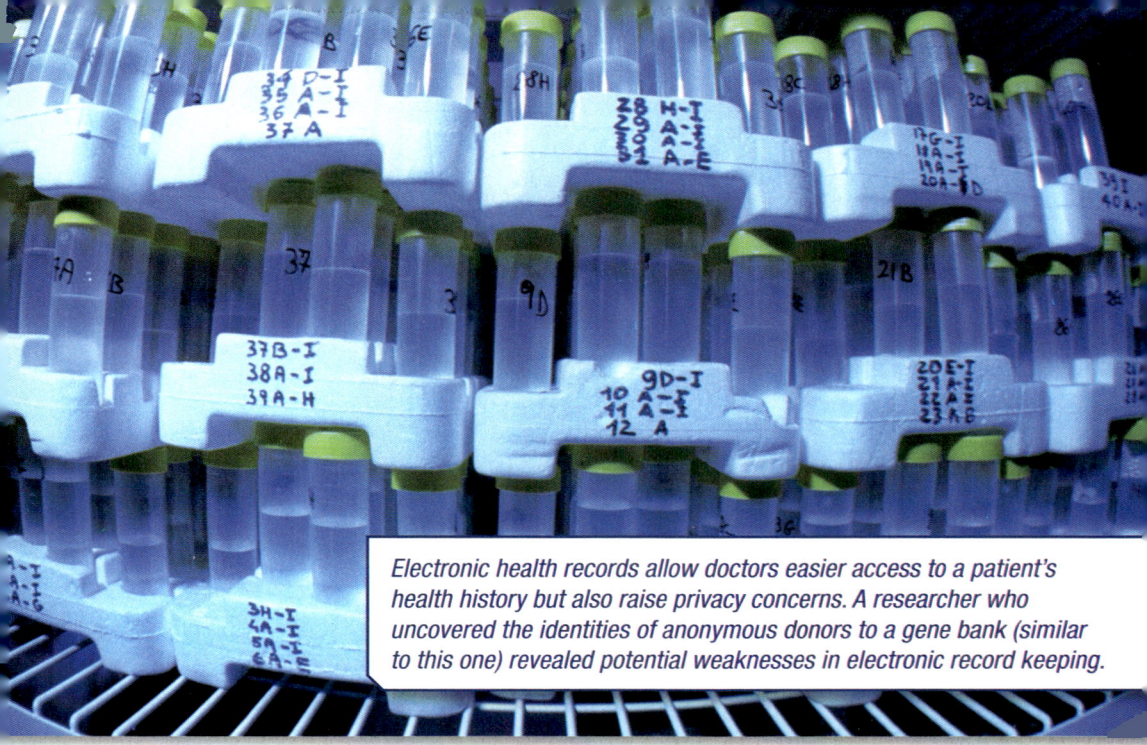

Electronic health records allow doctors easier access to a patient's health history but also raise privacy concerns. A researcher who uncovered the identities of anonymous donors to a gene bank (similar to this one) revealed potential weaknesses in electronic record keeping.

Things may actually prevent it from ever reaching the magnitude that is being predicted. Brookman says that "some poor design decisions today are compromising the revolutionary potential of the Internet of Things, with the potential result that many if not most consumers will reject many of these innovations."[43] That line of thinking was backed up by a January 2016 study by the consulting firm Accenture. The firm surveyed twenty-eight thousand respondents from twenty-eight countries. Nearly half cited concerns over security and privacy risks as top reasons they would avoid using devices and services in the Internet of Things.

Yet many others are convinced that the Internet of Things will one day be ubiquitous; that the time will come when *not* being connected is a rarity. Among them is *Forbes* contributor and author Jacob Morgan, who notes that in the future, "anything that can be connected, will be connected." The full implications of what all this interconnectivity will mean for individuals' online privacy remains to be seen and is only just beginning to be understood. "For now," says Morgan, "the best thing that we can do is educate ourselves about what the [Internet of Things] is and the potential impacts that can be seen on how we work and live."[44]

CHAPTER THREE

Privacy, Security, and Social Media

According to the market research group Smart Insights, more than 2 billion people worldwide were active social media users as of January 2016—nearly one-third of the global population. "Social media is the number one activity on the Web," says Jacob Silverman, author of *Terms of Service: Social Media and the Price of Constant Connection*. "There's nothing we spend more time doing online. One poll found that most British babies appear on social media within an hour of being born."[45]

Typically, people regard Facebook, Twitter, Tumblr, Instagram, and other social media platforms as fun and entertaining, and they can be. But the personal information users freely share on social media is also a treasure trove of data for anyone who profits by obtaining it. "Many people besides friends and acquaintances are interested in the information people post on social networks," says the Privacy Rights Clearinghouse. "Identity thieves, scam artists, debt collectors, stalkers, and corporations looking for a market advantage are using social networks to gather information about consumers."[46]

The Why and How of Collecting User Data

People who post on social media about their hobbies, activities, political affiliations, and latest family news may not see the value of this information. But it is extraordinarily valuable to companies whose success and profitability rely on fully understanding consumer wants and needs. Business Insider's senior research analyst Cooper Smith says that an immense amount of consumer data is generated through social media. "The average global Internet user spends two and a half hours daily on social media, and their activity reveals a great deal about what makes them tick," says Smith. He goes on to say that social media companies are making significant investments in putting user data to work. "If they achieve a firmer grip on users' relationships, interests, and spending habits," he says, "networks will be able to provide their users with personalized content, and advertisers will be able to hyper-target users."[47]

The methods social media sites and platforms use to collect user data often vary. As the largest and most popular social media site, Facebook has a monstrous database of user information that is collected as people socialize. This starts when users first open a Facebook account; they furnish their age, gender, and e-mail address, as well as other personal information. They create their timeline and start building their friends list, which further broadens their profile. Based on their personal choice, users may also give much more information, such as their hometown, schools they attended, their relationship status, employment history, and other details. Deeply personal information can be revealed through Facebook status updates, such as a divorce, someone entering drug rehab, or a scary medical diagnosis, as well as likes and shares, posts to friends' pages, and other activity. So the longer someone has been on Facebook, the larger and more detailed his or her profile will be—as well as valuable.

Twitter also collects data based on what its users tweet. Twitter's massive user database includes every user's personal information, such as age, who their followers are, and whom they follow. In November 2014 Twitter announced that it would also

> "Identity thieves, scam artists, debt collectors, stalkers, and corporations looking for a market advantage are using social networks to gather information about consumers."[46]
>
> —The Privacy Rights Clearinghouse, a consumer education and advocacy group that advocates for consumers' privacy rights.

track apps that are installed on users' mobile devices. This data collection, called App Graph, was ostensibly implemented so Twitter can more precisely tailor ad content for users. "Now, with the ability to peer into the apps that are installed on your mobile device," Sarah Perez writes in TechCrunch, "Twitter will also immediately have a better understanding of who a user is, and be able to customize that person's Twitter timeline with relevant content. That could potentially make for a more compelling Twitter experience, and ultimately draw users back to the network more often." If App Graph works as planned, Perez says it will allow Twitter to "grow and retain its user base of signed-in account holders, which translates into an improved bottom line."[48]

Privacy Statements: Long, Dull, and Often Ignored

When users first create a social media account, they are given a privacy statement that explains how the site or app will collect and use personal information. Yet it is very common for people to just skim through the statement or skip reading it altogether. This is largely because privacy statements tend to be long, complex, and hard to understand. In 2014, for instance, Facebook released an "abbreviated" version of its privacy policy that was twenty-seven hundred words in length—reduced from the original *nine thousand* words. "Aside from a few exceptions," says technology writer Kate Cox, "most privacy policies are utterly impenetrable for the average reader. They're long. They're dry. They're in a particularly tortuous form of legalese, designed to maximize corporate butt-covering and not consumer understanding. They're hard to find. And they're so ubiquitous and dull that we ignore them."[49]

> "Aside from a few exceptions, most privacy policies are utterly impenetrable for the average reader. They're long. They're dry. They're in a particularly tortuous form of legalese."[49]
>
> —Technology writer and editor Kate Cox.

If more social media users spent time reading privacy statements, they would likely be stunned at what they are freely giv-

> Billions of people enjoy sharing personal information on social media platforms such as Instagram (pictured). Many do not realize they are also providing a treasure trove of information to scam artists, identity thieves, stalkers, and others.

ing away. They would also become more aware of what privacy policies are and what they are not. According to a December 2014 survey by the Pew Research Center, more than half of Internet users believe that when a company posts a privacy policy, this ensures that user information is kept confidential. That is not true, however. Rather than serving as a protective mechanism for consumers, privacy policies are merely legal statements that disclose how customer data is managed and used. They say virtually nothing about the user's privacy being protected—and that is intentional. "We really don't know what kind of information we're giving over or how it's being used, and we have to accept the data collection regimes and the privacy standards for these companies," says Silverman. "It's either all or nothing. And we really have very little control."[50]

According to Nico Sell, the founder and CEO of the nonprofit privacy group Wickr Foundation, corporations have far more rights to social media users' data than most users realize. "I think people would be shocked to find out that almost every single privacy policy is the same," she says. "Whether it's WhatsApp,

Snapchat, Twitter, [or] Facebook you are granting a free transferable worldwide license for what you input into their free service."[51] Sell explains that this worldwide license means whatever users share on social media no longer belongs solely to them. Rather, by participating in social media, they have opted to share ownership and control of their personal information and photos with a corporation.

Captured Data

Even if social media users know their personal information is being captured, most are not aware that what they post or tweet can be sold to others. But the reality is, social media companies are businesses, and the operation of those businesses costs a great deal of money. Rather than users having to pay to participate, they agree (whether they know it or not) to have their personal information collected, used, and possibly sold to the highest bidder.

Theodore F. Claypoole, an intellectual property lawyer from Charlotte, North Carolina, says that social media companies are well aware of how closely their profits are tied to the personal information users are willing to share. In fact, according to Claypoole, the typical social media business model is designed to trick users into revealing profuse details about themselves. "Who are your friends?" he asks, "What discounts interest you? You 'liked' the last Vin Diesel movie, will you like the next one? What is your relationship status? Who do you write to? Who do you poke? Won't you download the mobile app so we can see where you are when you access our site? Your friends have downloaded our app. Why won't you? We will ask you again in two hours."[52]

The sale of users' personal information to third parties so companies can personalize their advertising to individuals is known as behavioral advertising, or targeting. Advertisers benefit from this practice because targeted ads are more likely to lead a viewer to

> "I think people would be shocked to find out that almost every single privacy policy is the same."[51]
>
> —Nico Sell, founder and CEO of the nonprofit privacy group Wickr Foundation.

Millennials Souring on Social Media

In June 2015, USA Network released a survey called "Nation Under A-Hack." Based on the survey's findings, a news release from the network presented an intriguing question: "Could a generation born and bred on social media and synonymous with 'selfie culture' be on the verge of a social shutdown?"

One thousand young adults participated in the survey. Its primary focus was to gauge millennials' attitudes and fears about computer hacking and cybercrime. One of the most insightful findings was related to their involvement in social media. More than half of respondents said that if they had the opportunity to start fresh, they would avoid joining social media altogether. When asked what they would do if major digital security breaches continue to occur, three-fourths of respondents said they were at least somewhat likely to deactivate their social media accounts. When asked about digital privacy, 78 percent said they were more concerned about it than they were a year ago. Yet nearly 70 percent of respondents felt they had no choice but to make their personal information available online.

NBCUniversal MediaVillage, "Are You Over the 'Selfie' Culture? Is the US in Danger of a Social Shutdown? Why Aren't Americans Doing More to Digitally Protect Themselves?," June 23, 2015. www.nbcumv.com.

---

purchase a product than a nontargeted ad. Social media users are often unconcerned about targeted advertising because they see no harm in it; after all, the ads they see are relevant to them. The practice, however, does raise concerns. For example, individuals are often not aware that their personal information is being gathered and sold—and this includes the personal information of minors. People also may not have the ability to view this data or correct any inaccuracies in it. In addition, such data may be held by the social media site and third parties indefinitely, and there may be very few safeguards in place to guard this data against hackers.

When Apps Gather Data

Third-party apps have become very popular on social media. These are applications that interact with but are not actually part of a social media site. Such third-party apps include online games (like FarmVille and Candy Crush Saga), quizzes (such as "Which Harry Potter Character Are You?" and "Which X-Men Villain Are You?"), and a variety of polls. These games and quizzes may be entertaining and make the social media site more exciting and creative, but they have a downside. When social media users click on these apps, they may wind up unknowingly sharing their personal information with the app company. Technology guru Kim Komando, who hosts a weekly radio program on digital issues, explains: "These third-party apps integrate with your Facebook profile and generally have permission to pull whatever information they want. And although you can edit what information they can access, very few people do."[53]

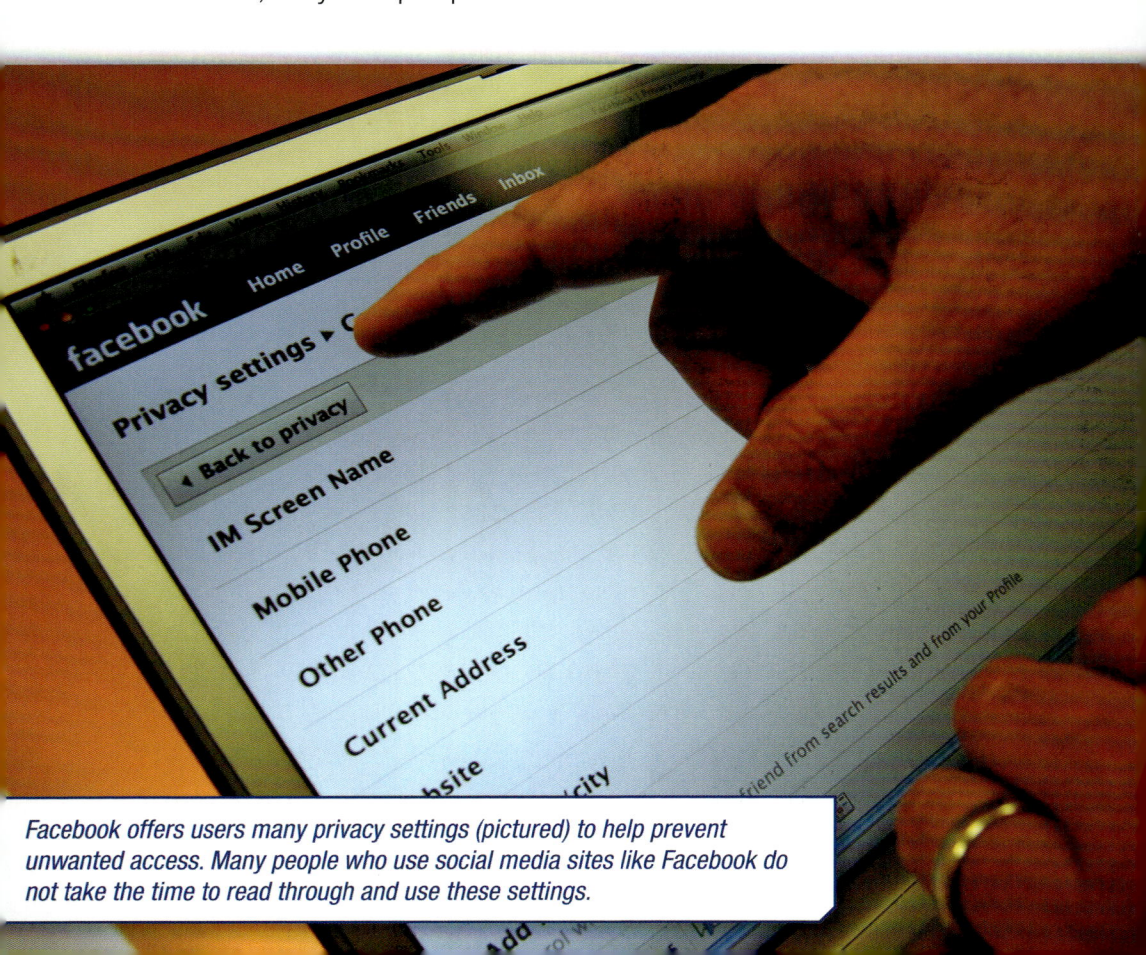

Facebook offers users many privacy settings (pictured) to help prevent unwanted access. Many people who use social media sites like Facebook do not take the time to read through and use these settings.

Security and privacy experts have been particularly critical of an app called Most Used Words on Facebook. "The app," says technology writer Paul Bischoff, "like many Facebook quiz apps, is a privacy nightmare."[54] In order to use the app, users must disclose personal information from their Facebook account, such as their friends list, the contents of their timeline, and all their photos. The app also allows Vonvon, the South Korean company that created it, to retain data about users even after they have stopped using the app. Within days of the app first appearing on Facebook, 16 million users had shared it on their pages. "That's over 16 million people," says Bischoff, "who agreed to give up almost every private detail about themselves to a company they likely know nothing about."[55] Bischoff adds that once user information has been captured by Vonvon, it could be stored anywhere in the world, including countries with weak or nonexistent privacy laws.

The Pew Research Center reports that apps now ask for more than two hundred different types of permission, including full access to a smartphone's Internet connection. Users may give permission for an app to access their public information, but most do not realize that third-party apps may also access some of their private information. In some instances, third-party apps may also access personal information of a user's contacts without obtaining permission from the contacts. Komando explains: "Even if you didn't download an app, your Facebook settings may allow apps your friends have installed to also see YOU."[56] A further concern is that these apps are not subject to the same privacy standards as the social media site itself. In fact, most of these sites do not take responsibility for the apps on their site, and some apps may contain malicious software (malware) such as a virus or Trojan horse.

> "Third-party apps integrate with your Facebook profile and generally have permission to pull whatever information they want. And although you can edit what information they can access, very few people do."[53]
>
> —Technology guru Kim Komando, who hosts a weekly radio program on digital issues.

Farming for Likes

When Facebook users "like" things their friends post on the site, it serves as an acknowledgment that they enjoyed, appreciated, and/or related to the post in some way. That small signal of approval also serves as a recommendation for others to read the post; and the more likes something has, the more often it becomes seen and shared with others. At first, this may sound like nothing more than an example of the "social" in social media. But it has led to a growing, troubling phenomenon known as "like farming," in which scammers trick people into clicking on a link that downloads malware onto their computers.

The scammers begin by posting an ordinary story, often one that appeals to users' emotions, on Facebook. Some of the most poignant and appealing of these posts show rescue animals and ask people to click the like button if they think the animals are cute. Komando explains:

> There are also the posts that ask for a like to show that you're against something the government is doing, or that you disagree with something terrible happening in the world. . . . Basically, any post that asks you to like it for emotional reasons, unless you know the person who created the original post, is quite probably a like-farm post.[57]

Other examples of like-farming posts are brain teasers such as tricky math problems and posts that claim users who click "like" will be eligible to win prizes such as an iPhone or gift cards.

Regardless of what tactic the post takes, when Facebook users like a story, it appears in their news feed, where their friends can view it and also click "like." As more and more people like the story—thereby spreading it around to a wider and wider viewing audience—the scammers up their game by inserting a malicious link in the story or by changing the story to something completely different. Once the page creators have accumulated hundreds of likes and shares, they may remove the page and begin promoting something entirely different, such as products they want to sell. The Better Business Bureau adds: "They may also sell the page and information that was collected from the 'likes' with a more direct threat of gaining access in an attempt to gather credit card numbers that may be stored for certain Facebook apps, passwords or other personal information."[58]

The simple act of clicking "like" to show appreciation for or enjoyment of an online post has opened the door to scammers who engage in "like farming." These scammers trick people into clicking on links that download malware onto their computers.

Intrusive Tracking

Some of the information a social media network collects on users is clear and obvious; for example, users must provide their date of birth and in most cases their real name in order to open the account. But other times, users are not aware what information the site is collecting from them. This information may be collected by using cookies to track where users go within the site, what links they click on, and which websites they visit after leaving the site. And many users are not aware that when they log on to other sites through Facebook, for example, the other site will get access to their Facebook profile information.

In March 2015 major media sources reported that because of Facebook's tracking practices in Europe, it was being investigated by officials in several European countries. Specifically, the investigation was triggered by Facebook's practice of tracking the online movements of users in order to sell targeted advertising. Government privacy watchdogs from France, Spain, and Italy, along with authorities from the Netherlands, Germany, and Belgium, alleged

Teens Post First, Ask Questions Later

Because the human brain is not fully developed until the early to mid-twenties, teens are more likely than adults to make impulsive, even unwise, decisions. According to a 2015 study by researchers from Penn State University, this includes the way in which young people use social media. The study showed that the way teens learn how to manage their privacy risk online is much different from how adults handle privacy management.

According to Haiyan Jia, a Penn State postdoctoral scholar who led the study, most adults think first, ask questions, and then act, whereas teens take risks first and then ask for help. This behavior is often hard for adults to understand, as Jia explains: "Adults . . . are so used to considering possible risks of disclosing information online first and then taking the necessary precautions, based on those concerns. What our model suggests is that teens don't think this way—they disclose and then evaluate the consequences. The process is more experiential in nature for teens."

The study revealed that teens are exposed to online privacy risks because of how they use social media: as a platform for self-expression and a way to be accepted by their peers. "Adults don't know how big of a deal [social media] is for teens," says Jia. "Before I worked on these papers, I was drawn to the issue because I heard about so many tragedies of teens who were exploring their identities online and that led them to very risky situations, often with terrible consequences." Since avoiding the Internet and social media is largely impossible for teens, it is essential that they become educated about being safe and guarding their privacy while online.

Quoted in Matt Swayne, "Teens' Approach to Social Media Risk Is Different from Adults," Penn State News, March 17, 2015. http://news.psu.edu.

that Facebook was tracking the computers of more than 300 million European citizens without their consent. This was happening whether or not users were logged on to Facebook—and also to people who visited Facebook and were not registered users of the site. Part of the investigation focused on the way Facebook combines data from its other services (such as Instagram and WhatsApp) to target advertising toward users. Also under investigation was how Facebook tracks users' Internet browsing habits by monitoring their use of the "like" button.

Growing Uncertainties

Privacy on social media has become one of the hottest topics in the technology world. Most users do not even think about the staggering amount of information they give away just by using social media. Even if they know their information is being collected, many have no idea that it is valuable enough to be bought and sold. As social media's popularity continues to grow and the number of users worldwide climbs even further, privacy concerns will undoubtedly become increasingly urgent.

Chapter Four

The Perils of Diminishing Online Privacy

Most people value their privacy but struggle to explain exactly why it is so important or why they should worry about protecting it. This is especially true of online privacy. A common view is that if someone has done nothing wrong and therefore has nothing to hide, what is there to be concerned about?

Constitutional lawyer and investigative journalist Glenn Greenwald, who is a fierce defender of privacy rights, hears this perspective all the time and is no longer surprised by it. So when he speaks at conferences and hears the inevitable statement "I don't really worry about invasions of privacy because I don't have anything to hide," Greenwald always responds the same way. He gets out a pen, writes down his e-mail address, hands it over, and tells the person:

> What I want you to do when you get home is email me the passwords to all of your email accounts, not just the nice, respectable work one in your name, but all of them, because I want to be able to just troll through what it is you're doing online, read what I want to read and publish whatever I find interesting. After all, if you're not a bad person, if you're doing nothing wrong, you should have nothing to hide.[59]

Not one person has ever taken Greenwald up on his offer. This does not surprise him, since he is convinced that people instinctively understand the profound importance of privacy. "There are all sorts of things that we do and think that we're willing to tell our physician or our lawyer or our psychologist or our spouse or our best friend that we would be mortified for the rest of the world to learn," says Greenwald. People regularly make decisions and judgments about what they are willing to share with others and what they want to keep to themselves. "People can very easily in words claim that they don't value their privacy," Greenwald writes, "but their actions negate the authenticity of that belief."[60]

> "People can very easily in words claim that they don't value their privacy, but their actions negate the authenticity of that belief."[60]
>
> —Glenn Greenwald, a constitutional lawyer and investigative journalist.

Why Privacy Is Important

Those who are apathetic about their online privacy may not understand just how valuable it really is—and they may not realize that until they have lost it. The most glaring problem with today's free-for-all collection of online information is that in a number of cases, people's rights are being violated. The US Constitution's Fourth Amendment states that "the right of the people to be secure in their persons, houses, papers, and effects, against unreasonable searches and seizures, shall not be violated." Even though that amendment was ratified more than two hundred years ago, constitutional law experts and privacy advocates emphasize that the same protection applies to people's online presence.

One expert is Mike Godwin, general counsel for the public policy research organization R. Street Institute. According to Godwin, e-mail that is stored for a long term on a server "is just as deserving of Fourth Amendment protections as letters locked away for years in a drawer."[61] Yet that is largely a matter of interpretation, since there is currently no legal protection of online privacy in the United States. The only existing law is the Electronic

Communications Privacy Act, which was passed in 1986—before the World Wide Web was even invented. Thus, the legislation is seriously outdated and inadequate for protecting citizens' online privacy rights.

Daniel Solove, a law professor at George Washington University Law School and an internationally known expert in privacy law, says that often, "courts and commentators struggle to articulate why privacy is so valuable. They see privacy violations as often slight annoyances, but privacy matters a lot more than that." One of the most important reasons why privacy matters so much is that it limits government power. Someone who has been arrested, for instance, and whose case was dropped because of no evidence, will still have data showing the arrest. "In the wrong hands," says Solove, "personal data can be used to cause us great harm."[62]

Along with keeping power in check, privacy is also essential for safeguarding freedom of thought and speech. People need to feel free to read whatever books and magazines they want and watch whatever programs they want without fear that they are being watched by the government. Also, privacy enables people to speak their minds freely. "We may want to criticize people we know to others yet not share that criticism with the world," says Solove. Or, he adds, someone "might want to explore ideas that their family or friends or colleagues dislike."[63]

Sharing and Oversharing

The freedom to be able to speak one's mind is an integral part of people's sharing on social media. In fact, the word *share* has taken on a whole new meaning. Whereas in the past, when sharing typically meant a selfless, generous act (such as sharing one's good fortune with others), sharing is widely used today in reference to what is posted or tweeted on social media. "Sharing used to be something we did in school when there weren't enough textbooks to go around," says CNN Digital producer Brandon Griggs. "Then came Facebook, and everyone—not just the generous—became sharers. . . . Share buttons popped up all over the Web. Share this! Tweet this! Pin this! Snap this! Sooo much sharing."[64]

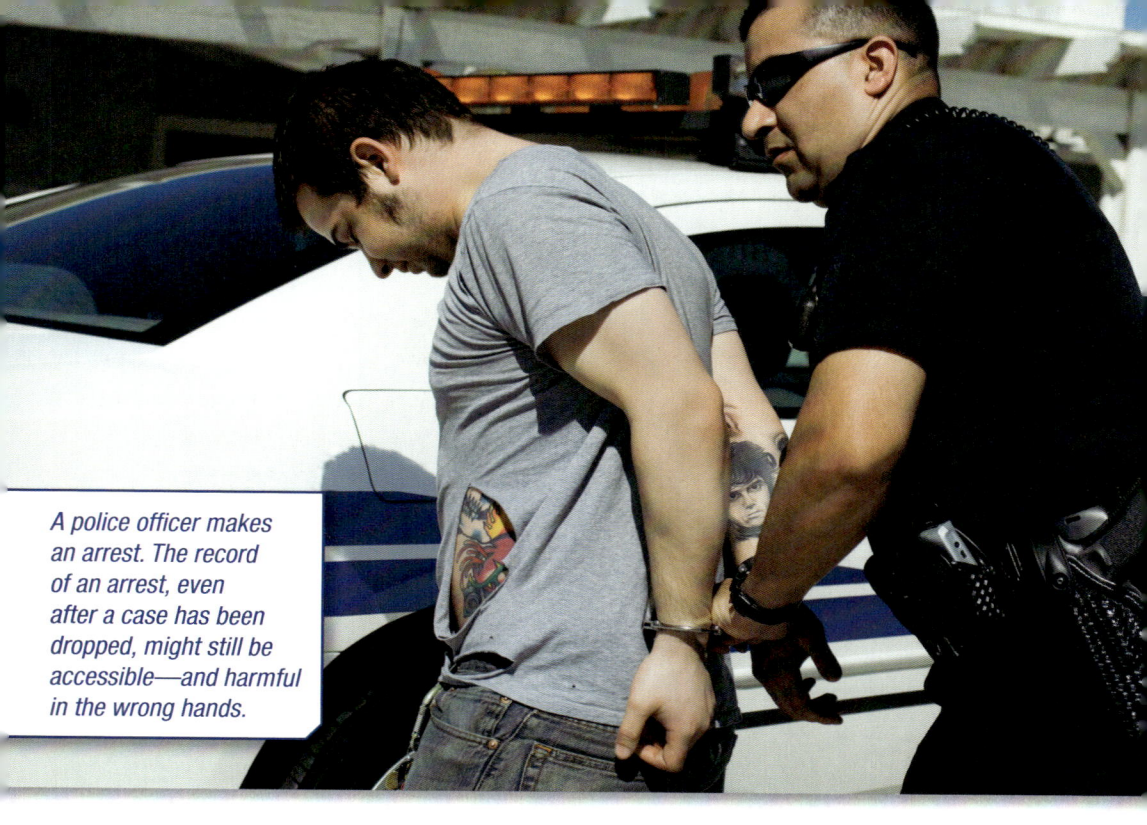

A police officer makes an arrest. The record of an arrest, even after a case has been dropped, might still be accessible—and harmful in the wrong hands.

In the process of sharing on social media, people often forget that everything they say and do online is public information—even if they intend it only for their friends or followers. "A problematic feature of social media is that we can't physically see or hear the large number of people we're 'talking' to," says Nancy Rothbard, a management professor at the Wharton School of the University of Pennsylvania. She adds that social media interactions are characterized by open disclosure to broad audiences, some of which are not visible. "So," says Rothbard, "we tend to forget that this invisible audience is present: dozens, even hundreds, of people are reading our posts and forming judgments about us."[65]

It is extraordinarily common for people to "overshare," meaning they reveal too much information in their posts or tweets. Another common mistake among social media users is forgetting that once something is posted or tweeted, it remains online forever. Online news publications are brimming with stories of people who post things that come back to haunt them later in life. "Sharing the wrong thing on social media can cost people their jobs, or even their careers and professional reputation,"[66] says Rothbard.

The Price of Indiscretion

A growing number of businesses and corporations monitor applicants' social media presence to learn as much as possible about a potential employee. A common reason employers do this is to determine whether someone would present a good image for their organization. "Part of what companies do when they [search] for you on social media is to see how you conduct yourself," says Marcie Kirk Holland, a project manager at the University of California–Davis Internship and Career Center. "They want to know how you'll interact with your co-workers and more importantly their customers or potential customers."[67]

After people land a job, they also need to be careful what they say online, especially about their boss or coworkers. For example, an employee who is angry with his or her boss or a client may be tempted to write a scathing post or tweet on social media, but this is not wise. Human resources consultant Brenda Vander Meulen cautions, "Never say anything negative about a current or former employer on your social media pages. Employers will reasonably assume that if you trash-talk your current or former employers, they will be the next ones to be trashed."[68]

She also reminds employees to use common sense and not post photos of themselves partying or write about calling in sick to go out with friends.

In July 2014 a waitress at a restaurant in Findlay, Ohio, was fired after pouring out her frustration on Facebook. On a Friday night after making only $60 in tips, Kirsten Kelly was angry. "More than one time," she says, "people spent $50 or more and they tipped five or six (dollars). That's not OK!" Later that evening, Kelly logged on to Facebook and posted: "If you come into a restau-

> "Sharing the wrong thing on social media can cost people their jobs, or even their careers and professional reputation."[66]
>
> —Nancy Rothbard, a management professor at the Wharton School of the University of Pennsylvania.

Phony Families

When a Charlotte, North Carolina, woman named Jenny noticed a sudden surge in new Instagram followers, she became suspicious. Then she received two private messages, both of which were confusing as well as disturbing. The messages alerted Jenny that a photo of her baby daughter was being displayed by an Instagram user named Nikki, who claimed the baby was hers. That was when Jenny discovered she was a victim of a growing and alarming baby role-playing community on Instagram. Players find photos of babies and young children that are displayed on the site, choose the ones they want to "adopt," and copy the photos without the parents' knowledge or permission. Once the photo is in place, role-playing begins. In some cases Instagrammers play the role of virtual adoption agencies. Followers can request specific babies they want to "adopt," and the virtual agency will find photos that match their desired characteristics.

This type of activity violates Instagram's terms of service, and once a parent or guardian reports it, the company claims that it quickly removes the photos. Yet this has proved to be untrue. When Jenny contacted Instagram, she became frustrated at the company's inability to understand the problem or take steps to help her. The experience has made her much more judicious about what she posts on the Internet, especially when it comes to photos of her children.

---

rant and spend $50 or more, you should be able to tip appropriately for that."[69] Although Kelly kept her post vague and did not name any customers, one of them (a Facebook friend) saw the post, printed out a screenshot of it, and took it to Kelly's managers, who promptly fired her.

Putting Kids at Risk

Even when people are careful about what they say online, they can still cause problems for themselves. For example, parents often share pictures and personal details about their children's lives on social media—and studies show that this may put their children at risk. Many parents who post photos on social media sites such as Facebook, Twitter, and Instagram inadvertently overshare. "On one hand, social media offers today's parents an outlet they find incredibly useful," says Sarah J. Clark, a pediatric researcher at the University of Michigan's C.S. Mott Children's Hospital. "On the other hand, some are concerned that oversharing may pose safety and privacy risks for their children."[70]

Some parents have been shocked to find that pictures they posted of their children have been copied and used on pages of unknown social media users without permission. This may never lead to problems, but for the parents involved, it feels like a

When parents post photographs of their children on social media, they may inadvertently be exposing them to exploitation. Some parents have been shocked to find those photos used on unfamiliar sites without permission.

creepy invasion of privacy. Also, for young people whose photos have been plastered all over their parents' social media pages, this may lead to embarrassment when they are teens. Child psychologist Yalda T. Uhls says that her daughter, who is now fifteen, asked to have a photo taken off Facebook that showed Uhls kissing her because she was embarrassed by it. "My first reaction was, 'I don't have to do that, it's my photo and it's sweet,'" says Uhls. "But then I realized that she had every right to ask me, so I took it down."[71]

In 2015 researchers at the New York University Polytechnic School of Engineering and NYU Shanghai showed the extent to which parents compromise their children's privacy by posting photos for anyone to see. The researchers sifted through the social media profiles of twenty-four hundred adults in an East Coast town to find parents who had posted photos of their children. The team combined these social media profiles with public records, such as voter registrations, to find the parents' home addresses. Then, using facial recognition software and comments on the photos, the researchers were able to deduce personal information about the children, such as their full names, addresses, and date of birth.

Project lead Tehila Minkus explains that the goal of the research "was not to publicly expose sensitive information about children, but rather to raise awareness about the results of oversharing."[72] Parental oversharing can make children the target of identity thieves, who would be armed with enough information to glean a child's Social Security number; or kidnappers, who could figure out a child's address. Not only does parental oversharing put these children's safety, privacy, and identity at risk, but it also makes it harder—even impossible—for the children to protect their own online privacy in the future.

> "On one hand, social media offers today's parents an outlet they find incredibly useful. On the other hand, some are concerned that oversharing may pose safety and privacy risks for their children."[70]
>
> —Sarah J. Clark, a pediatric researcher at the University of Michigan's C.S. Mott Children's Hospital.

The Threat of Widespread Surveillance

It is not only identity thieves, kidnappers, and hackers who pose a threat to online privacy. The US government has also been accused of violating citizens' privacy online—and because of a man named Edward Snowden, the government was caught red-handed. A former contract systems analyst for the National Security Agency (NSA), Snowden did something in May 2013 that led some people to call him a traitor deserving of prison and others to hail him as a national hero.

While contracting with the NSA, Snowden secretly downloaded classified NSA documents, which he later released to his trusted source, Glenn Greenwald. In doing so, Snowden blew the whistle on a massive, warrantless, US government surveillance operation that lasted for more than a decade. Snowden revealed, says Greenwald, that the United States and several other countries secretly used the Internet as an "unprecedented zone of mass, indiscriminate surveillance."[73]

The information Snowden leaked showed that the government was regularly violating the privacy rights of US citizens by monitoring Internet traffic and storing private data. Because he released classified documents, Snowden had to flee to Russia to avoid prosecution in the United States. But the documents he exposed helped raise global awareness not only of government surveillance, but also online privacy. Steve Wozniak, who along with Steve Jobs founded Apple Computer, refers to Snowden as a "total hero" because what he did has helped protect people's constitutional rights. Wozniak has lauded Snowden for acting "from his own heart, his own belief in the United States Constitution, what democracy and freedom was about." Wozniak adds, "And now a federal judge has said that NSA data collection was unconstitutional."[74]

One area of concern is that the government could use people's own devices to spy on them. In fact, in February 2016 James Clapper, US director of national intelligence, stated during congressional testimony that it was possible US government agencies would step up their surveillance of people by using smart devices such as cell phones, cars, and even dishwashers. Ac-

Edward Snowden (photographed during a 2013 interview) downloaded and released thousands of classified National Security Agency documents. His actions revealed widespread government surveillance of US citizens and others.

cording to Clapper, "In the future, intelligence services might use the [Internet of Things] for identification, surveillance, monitoring, location tracking, and targeting for recruitment, or to gain access to networks or user credentials."[75] Although he did not name any specific intelligence agency, his words sparked concern among security experts, privacy advocates, and private citizens. Yet many people who own smart devices remain unaware that the government may use the Internet of Things as part of a mass surveillance program.

In fact, the Internet of Things is already being used by law enforcement agencies, which have used court orders to compel tech companies to turn over data they have gathered from their users—data that the users may not even be aware they are transmitting. For example, police have asked Dropcam, which is owned by Google, to turn over footage from webcams people have installed in their homes. Many people have become aware—thanks to the publicity generated by the enormous public backlash—that Samsung Smart TVs pick up everything that is said in a room and transmit it back to the company. But what many people do not know is that plenty of other devices and services do the same thing. This includes other TV models, Xbox Kinect, Amazon Echo, and the OnStar program

Is Your Data Wrong?

Acxiom is one of the largest data brokers in the United States, with a database that holds personal information on several hundred million people. In 2013 the company launched a website called AboutTheData.com, where consumers can enter their name to see what information Acxiom has collected on them, such as their political beliefs, race, income, and personal interests. In many cases, however, this information is inaccurate. People have found minor mistakes in their phone number or e-mail address. Others have found more significant mistakes, such as the wrong occupation, income, or level of education. For example, in 2013 ten employees of CNN Money checked their profiles, and each of them found at least one significant mistake—and some found multiple errors. These included household income, level of education, and whether they had children, as well as the wrong ethnicity, which is deduced based on a person's surname.

Jonathan Mayer of Stanford University's Center for Internet and Society thinks data brokers such as Acxiom need to take more care that the information they gather about people is correct. Mayer says that when he checked his own profile, he found that Acxiom had most of his information wrong. "I was pegged as a motorcycling Christian who owns a Nissan Pathfinder and, I think, had two or three kids, all of which is entirely incorrect," says Mayer. "This certainly raises some questions about how useful is this really, if the data is so messy."

Quoted in Chris Gaylord, "AboutTheData.com Asks If You Recognize Your Online Self," *Christian Science Monitor*, March 1, 2014. www.csmonitor.com.

in GM vehicles. There is even a Barbie doll that responds to voices to have a "conversation" with people but also transmits everything it hears back to toy company Mattel. Trevor Trimm, executive director of the nonprofit Freedom of the Press Foundation, shares his thoughts: "While people voluntarily use all these devices, the chances are close to zero that they fully understand that a lot of their data is being sent back to various companies to be stored on servers that can either be accessed by governments or hackers."[76]

A Hot Topic

Anja Kaspersen, who heads Geopolitics and International Security at the World Economic Forum, is among those who are concerned about the intrusive government surveillance of private citizens. Kaspersen acknowledges that a great challenge in the coming years will be ensuring protection "while retaining the critical underpinnings of our democratic systems—free speech, freedom of assembly and association, and, critically, the right to privacy."[77]

Indeed, online privacy is fast disappearing, although people are often oblivious to that fact. They post their thoughts and opinions, upload photos, fire off tweets, or share their frustrations without thinking twice about the potential risks. Those who are confronted by how their privacy is disappearing often have no idea why this should concern them. Many even feel apathetic about widespread government surveillance, believing that since they have nothing to hide, they have nothing to lose. Perhaps when people become fully aware of how their privacy is slipping away, they may start caring more and take steps to guard it.

CHAPTER FIVE

Protecting Online Privacy

On October 8, 2015, California governor Jerry Brown signed into law an act that was hailed as the nation's most comprehensive, and toughest, online privacy legislation. With implementation of the California Electronic Communications Privacy Act (CalECPA), law enforcement and investigation agencies are prohibited from asking any business to turn over digital communications without a warrant. This includes e-mails, text messages, and all documents stored in the cloud. The law also requires a warrant to track the location of electronic devices such as mobile phones or to search them. "This is a landmark win for digital privacy and all Californians," says Nicole Ozer, technology and civil liberties policy director at the ACLU of California. "We hope this is a model for the rest of the nation in protecting our digital privacy rights."[78]

Also expressing support for the law are the Electronic Frontier Foundation and major technology companies like Apple, Google, Facebook, Dropbox, LinkedIn, and Twitter, all of which are headquartered in California. These companies, along with privacy advocates and citizens, think that much more needs to be done to protect online privacy, and the first place to start is with the law.

Much-Needed Legislation

Although five other US states require a warrant for content, and nine require a warrant for GPS tracking, California's law is the first to enable protections for location data, metadata, content, and device searches. The many individuals and groups who are enthusiastic about the California law say it is long overdue, because secretive surveillance programs have become more prolific in the state. For example, according to journalist and privacy advocate Cory Doctorow, police officers in Oakland, California, use license cams that track drivers' moves within city limits. Doctorow calls these "secretive automatic license plate readers" and says they show that the Oakland Police Department "has mounted a program of incredibly intrusive, highly racialized secret surveillance of an entire city."[79]

Also widely used by law enforcement in California are surveillance gadgets known as stingrays. These track residents' locations by covertly spying on their cell phones. The suitcase-sized stingrays are known for their ability to pinpoint a target with extraordinary precision. In January 2016 the Anaheim Police Department acknowledged that it had been using stingrays known as dirtboxes that are mounted on low-flying aircraft. This surveillance technique allows law enforcement to surveil entire regions simultaneously and is regarded as very intrusive. "This cell phone spying program—which potentially affects the privacy of everyone from Orange County's 3 million residents to the 16 million people who visit Disneyland every year—shows the dangers of allowing law enforcement to secretly acquire surveillance technology,"[80] argues ACLU technology and civil liberties policy attorney Matt Cagle.

Because of these and other tactics that threaten people's privacy rights, California's privacy law was a welcome announcement. California state senators Mark Leno and Joel Anderson cowrote the law with the aim of giving digital data the same protections as nondigital communications. As Leno explains, "For too long, California's digital privacy laws have been stuck in the Dark Ages, leaving our personal emails, text messages, photos and smartphones increasingly vulnerable to warrantless searches. That ends today."[81]

> "For too long, California's digital privacy laws have been stuck in the Dark Ages, leaving our personal emails, text messages, photos and smartphones increasingly vulnerable to warrantless searches."[81]
>
> —Mark Leno, a California state senator.

As someone who frequently writes about privacy issues and threats to privacy, Doctorow was also happy about the new law—but he does not think the matter should end there. "Now it's time to get [CalECPA's] equivalents passed in the other 49 states," says Doctorow, "and then made federal law."[82]

Updating an Antiquated Law

Numerous privacy advocates share Doctorow's belief. The only federal law that is currently on the books, the Electronic Communications Privacy Act, was originally passed in 1986, so it is seriously dated. Under that law, information stored on a server—as is the case with information on social media—can be easily accessed by the government or law enforcement through a subpoena. Many industries and advocates are working to strengthen the act by requiring government and law enforcement to obtain a search warrant.

According to the Center for Democracy & Technology (CDT), when the original privacy law was written, it was a "forward-looking statute"[83] that provided important privacy protections to people who were using first-generation cell phones and the early Internet. In the years following the law's passage, however, technology evolved dramatically—but the statute's privacy standards did not keep pace. As a result, privacy experts say, important information lacked full protection. "Meanwhile," says the CDT, "the courts have been slow in extending the warrant requirement of the Constitution's Fourth Amendment to new technologies."[84] The federal government, therefore, technically has the power to track citizens' movements without a warrant by using their cell phones, which continuously report locations to wireless service providers. And, says the CDT, the government has maintained the position that it does not need a warrant to read people's e-mails or other documents that are stored and shared privately in the cloud. Privacy organizations believe otherwise, however.

In April 2016 the House Judiciary Committee unanimously approved legislation called the Email Privacy Act (H.R. 699), which would reform the 1986 law. H.R. 699 establishes the first federal statute requiring a uniform warrant for stored communica-

In 2015, Governor Jerry Brown of California (pictured) signed into law the California Electronic Communications Privacy Act. This act has been described as the nation's toughest and most comprehensive online privacy legislation.

tion content in all criminal investigations. It brings an end to the 1986 law's arbitrary 180-day rule, which permits e-mail communications to be obtained without a warrant after 180 days. "The core of H.R. 699 is a significant reform," says Bob Goodlatte, chair of the House Judiciary Committee. "It establishes a standard that embodies the principles of the Fourth Amendment and reaffirms our commitment to protecting the privacy interests of the American people."[85] The bill was advanced to the full House of Representatives on April 13, 2016, for a vote, and the House unanimously passed it by the end of that month. From there it was forwarded to the US Senate for a vote. As of June 2016 the Senate had taken no action on the bill.

Additional Legislative Efforts

Other proposed federal legislation includes an automotive security bill introduced in 2015 by Senators Ed Markey and Richard Blumenthal. The bill seeks to direct the NHTSA to set mandatory cybersecurity and consumer privacy standards for self-driving cars. "We need enforceable rules of the road to protect driver privacy and security,"[86] Markey stated during a hearing on the new technology in March 2016. Representatives from auto and tech companies—including Google, Delphi Automotive, and GM—who attended the hearing declined to comment on whether they would support the bill, although the representatives for GM and Delphi said they were willing to work with regulators if such standards were to be enacted.

Also in 2015, the FTC released a report that recommended ways to safeguard user privacy in the Internet of Things. It encouraged companies to build security features into devices from the outset and at every stage of development, rather than as an afterthought. The FTC also said that companies should require consumers to change default passwords when consumers set up their smart devices (which is good practice, but not currently a requirement). Among other recommendations were that companies should minimize the amount of personal data they collect and store and test their security features before launching a product. The report states, "Such testing should occur because companies—and service providers they might use to help develop their products—may simply forget to close 'backdoors' in their products through which intruders could access personal information or gain control of the device."[87]

The FTC also stressed how important it is for companies to train their employees on security measures and make sure such measures have oversight from managers. Companies should also make sure that the service providers they use follow reasonable security measures. The report discussed how many companies do not currently do this and cited as an example GMR Transcription Services, a medical and legal transcription company that outsourced work to a company in India but did not make sure the company used adequate security measures. The FTC found that the service provider in India stored unencrypted notes on an un-

> "We need enforceable rules of the road to protect driver privacy and security."[86]
>
> —Ed Markey, a US senator from Massachusetts.

Privacy: An Essential Right

Surveys have shown that many people have little to no awareness of how much personal information they divulge online—and how valuable that information is to those who buy and sell it. Even more disturbing to security and privacy experts is that when people learn about their eroding online privacy, they are often unconcerned.

Jamie Bartlett, a social media analyst from the United Kingdom, wants people to understand how vital their personal privacy is and how important it is to guard it. Bartlett offers examples of how people in some of the world's most hostile regions put their lives on the line to protect their privacy:

> Syrian democrats really do create secret and untraceable chat rooms to coordinate activity. Russian dissidents really do use internet browsers like Tor to circumnavigate state censorship of the net. Homosexuals in the Middle East really do use encryption to avoid a knock at the door from brutal enforcers of state morality. Anonymising tools like the Tor browser has had a hugely beneficial effect on free expression around the world.

Bartlett emphasizes that privacy is essential not only in the most hostile parts of the world, but also for people everywhere. "Well-established democracies use secret ballots to ensure that people can express their political views without hindrance or fear," he says. "There are many ways that privacy contributes to free expression." According to Bartlett, the ability to remain anonymous online is a key factor in protecting online privacy. "Genuine anonymity has and does grant people the space to speak their mind, to push boundaries, to propel society forward."

Jamie Bartlett, "How We All Became Obsessed with Online Privacy," *Telegraph* (London), June 16, 2015. www.telegraph.co.uk.

---

secured server, which resulted in doctors' notes about the physical exams of US patients being freely available on the Internet.

The report also recommended that companies monitor devices and provide security patches to cover known security risks;

employ multiple layers of security to defend against security risks; and take measures to prevent unauthorized users from accessing a user's device, data, or personal information that is stored on a server or social media site. The purpose of these efforts is to help individuals trust that the government, industries, and online platforms will protect their privacy and safety. Says FTC chair Edith Ramirez, "The only way for the Internet of Things to reach its full potential for innovation is with the trust of American consumers."[88]

State Action

Privacy protection laws are also being aggressively pursued by the states. By mid-2016 all but three US states—Alabama, New Mexico, and South Dakota—had laws that require consumers to be notified of any security breaches that involve personal information. These laws apply to businesses, governments, and educational institutions. In addition, at least twenty-five states had introduced or were considering amendments to their security breach notification bills or resolutions.

The proposed changes include expanding the definition of "personal information" to include medical, insurance, or biometric data, as well as expanding or redefining who must comply with a state's notification laws. For example, in Florida, Governor Rick Scott signed a bill on March 25, 2016, that provides for computer security incident response teams, mandates training programs, requires risk assessments, and requires notification of data security breaches. And in Illinois, Governor Bruce Rauner signed a bill on May 6, 2016, to amend the state's Personal Information Protection Act to include breaches of security that involve EHRs, health insurance information, and online accounts.

Transparency Is Key

In order for social media sites, industry, and the government to earn and keep people's trust, such groups must be very forthright in explaining how they go about protecting the privacy rights of individuals. This is known as transparency. According to Rami Essaid, CEO of cybersecurity company Distil Networks, total trans-

One of Google's self-driving cars, parked on Pennsylvania Avenue in Washington, DC, awaits its next journey. Members of Congress have considered a bill that would set mandatory cybersecurity and consumer privacy standards for self-driving cars.

parency is the only feasible answer to the seemingly insurmountable online privacy issue. "The world is engaged in the wrong conversation when it comes to Internet privacy," says Essaid. "Tracking happens—get over it. The conversation we should be having isn't about absolute privacy . . . but about transparency."[89]

One of the ways companies can be more transparent, according to Essaid, is to make sure every site makes clear to users what he calls the "Five W's" of tracking: "Who is tracking me, what are they doing with the information, where, when and why?" He also recommends:

> Rather than today's often-impenetrable privacy statements, companies should publish a detailed, dumbed-down description of their tracking procedures. When you visit a website, who is that website sharing its data with? Facebook, for example, could avoid its European problem if it simply disclosed what data it collects, what it does with that data, with whom they share it, and what those others do with it.[90]

What Individuals Can Do

Many people feel like protecting their online privacy is out of their hands; that their only protection will come from tougher regulations. But security and privacy experts emphasize that individuals have far greater ability to protect themselves while online than they realize.

This is especially true for social media users. For example, Twitter users can uncheck the "Add a location to my Tweets" box in their account's security and privacy settings to opt out of the geotagging feature and hide their location. Social media users can also scrutinize their account settings to find out which outside apps can access or post to their accounts. Users can then decide whether to allow or revoke access for each app they find listed. One of the most important measure individuals can take to guard their privacy online is to manage who has access to their social media sites such as Facebook and Instagram. Users are advised to restrict their accounts so that only select groups of people can read their posts and see their photos.

> "The world is engaged in the wrong conversation when it comes to Internet privacy. Tracking happens—get over it."[89]
>
> —Rami Essaid, CEO of cybersecurity company Distil Networks.

Another step people can take to protect their privacy is to delete their search history and cookies on a regular basis. Also, enabling the "Do not track" feature on web browsers lets consumers opt out of third-party web tracking. This feature is relatively unknown among Internet users; surveys have shown that only a small percentage of users have taken advantage of it. For the more technologically savvy users, browser plug-ins such as Ghostery or Disconnect.me can help pinpoint the hundreds of sites that are tracking a user at any given moment.

Aimee Picchi, a business writer for CBS MoneyWatch, shares some tips on other ways consumers can guard their privacy. For instance, when an app wants to do something that requires permission, it says something to the user like, "Twitter would like to access your photos." According to Picchi, users should con-

Going Low-Tech to Protect Online Privacy

When asked about online privacy, many people say that there is not much they can do to protect it. But according to CNBC tech reporter Harriet Taylor, there are many low-tech ways individuals can do just that. For example, Taylor recommends that people put a piece of tape or a sticker over the webcam in their phones, tablets, and Smart TVs to prevent hackers from using the devices to spy on them. Similarly, to prevent hackers from turning on the microphone in a smartphone to use the phone as a listening device, users can simply plug their headphone into the device. Some people even cut the cord off an old headphone and plug just the jack into the phone.

When conducting a search online, Taylor recommends that individuals practice self-censorship. Because search engines such as Google sell keywords from searches to advertisers, people should avoid searching for highly sensitive information, such as questions about health issues. For questions such as these, says Taylor, people should consult their doctor. Another way to guard one's privacy when searching online is to use an Internet search engine that does not collect data on users, such as DuckDuckGo. Nico Sell, cofounder of the encrypted messaging service Wickr and organizer of the Def Con hacker conference, goes a step further to prevent data brokers from building a profile of her to use for targeted advertising. When using a search engine, Sell will throw in a search for something completely out of character. "I often do searches for chainsaws, I also put into Google Maps wrong addresses just to gum up the system," says Sell.

Quoted in Harriet Taylor, "Ten Low-Tech Ways to Protect Your Privacy Online," CNBC, June 22, 2015. www.cnbc.com.

sider declining the request. Consumers on iPhones can also get into their settings to look at different apps' permissions, and then check off the ones that they do not want to give. "It's also important to check the privacy tab in settings to review what different

> "Unless we insist on new rules to govern and regulate the use of these new technologies, it's not only our privacy that will be lost, but all that depends on privacy as well—including democracy itself."[93]
>
> —David Cole, a professor at Georgetown University Law Center

apps are able to tap, such as your contacts or location,"[91] says Picchi.

Experts stress that one of the most important things consumers can do to protect themselves and their privacy is to refrain from oversharing online. For example, people should never give out their date of birth on social media, nor should they reveal their hometown or where they went to high school or college. Information like this is coveted by identity thieves. "You may call into a call center or reset a password to verify who you are. They may ask what is your birthdate," says computer security expert Bill Dean of Sword and Shield Enterprises. "We want to share everything, but we don't realize it's like bread crumbs that someone can put together and create a new identity or use to know much more about us than we want people to know."[92]

Future Uncertainties

How to best protect citizens' privacy rights, and help them protect themselves, is an issue of utmost importance; one that is being tackled by privacy and security experts, advocacy organizations, and lawmakers at all levels. This is no easy task, but it is essential because more than ever before, privacy is threatened. "Privacy has never been more vulnerable than it is today," says Georgetown University Law Center professor David Cole. "The digital era has brought us many delightful conveniences, but it has simultaneously created previously unthinkable perils." Cole argues that even though privacy is not yet dead, "it may be on life support. And unless we insist on new rules to govern and regulate the use of these new technologies, it's not only our privacy that will be lost, but all that depends on privacy as well—including democracy itself."[93]

SOURCE NOTES

Introduction: A Slow, Steady Loss

1. Quoted in Matthew Panzarino, "Apple's Tim Cook Delivers Blistering Speech on Encryption, Privacy," TechCrunch, June 2, 2015. http://techcrunch.com.
2. Quoted in Panzarino, "Apple's Tim Cook Delivers Blistering Speech on Encryption, Privacy."
3. Quoted in Jeffrey Brown, "How Can We Return Privacy Control to Social Media Users?," *PBS NewsHour*, April 7, 2015. www.pbs.org.
4. Quoted in Panzarino, "Apple's Tim Cook Delivers Blistering Speech on Encryption, Privacy."
5. Quoted in Natasha Singer, "Sharing Data, but Not Happily," *New York Times*, June 4, 2015. www.nytimes.com.
6. Joseph Turow, Michael Hennessy, and Nora Draper, "The Tradeoff Fallacy," report from the Annenberg School for Communication, University of Pennsylvania, June 2015. www.asc.upenn.edu.
7. Quoted in Tom Risen, "The Illusion of Online Privacy," *U.S. News & World Report*, August 25, 2015. www.usnews.com.

Chapter One: The Digital Trail

8. Quoted in *Frontline*, "Podcast: How to Protect Yourself (and Your Data) Online," PBS, May 20, 2014. www.pbs.org.
9. Quoted in Steve Henn, "If There's Privacy in the Digital Age, It Has a New Definition," WBUR News, March 3, 2014. www.wbur.org.
10. Quoted in Jeffrey Brown, "Companies Tracking Our Online Footsteps Should Be More Transparent, Says FTC," *PBS NewsHour*, June 13, 2014. www.pbs.org.
11. Mark Stockley, "Anatomy of a Browser Dilemma—How HSTS 'Supercookies' Make You Choose Between Privacy or Security," *Naked Security* (blog), Sophos, February 2, 2015. https://nakedsecurity.sophos.com.
12. Panda Security, "How Do Cookies Work?," October 8, 2014. www.pandasecurity.com.
13. Timothy L. Warner, "Protect Your Online Privacy by Removing Exif Data from Your Photos," Que Publishing, May 15, 2014. www.quepublishing.com.
14. Quoted in Tyler Cohen Wood, "How Social Media Exposes Us to Predators and Other Online Bottom-Feeders [Excerpt]," *Scientific American*, April 18, 2014. www.scientificamerican.com.

15. Quoted in Jose Pagliery, "'Super Cookies' Track You, Even in Privacy Mode," CNNMoney, January 9, 2015. http://money.cnn.com.
16. Privacy Rights Clearinghouse, "Online Privacy: Using the Internet Safely," January 2016. www.privacyrights.org.
17. Quoted in Brown, "Companies Tracking Our Online Footsteps Should Be More Transparent, Says FTC."
18. Jacob Silverman, *Terms of Service: Social Media and the Price of Constant Connection*. New York: HarperCollins, 2015, p. 214.
19. Quoted in Steve Kroft, "The Data Brokers: Selling Your Personal Information," CBS News, August 24, 2014. www.cbsnews.com.
20. Quoted in Kroft, "The Data Brokers."
21. Adam Tanner, "How Data Brokers Make Money Off Your Medical Records," *Scientific American*, February 1, 2016. www.scientificamerican.com.
22. Sherbit, "Facebook Partners with Shadowy 'Data Brokers' to Farm Your Information," April 16, 2015. www.sherbit.io.
23. Federal Trade Commission, "Data Brokers: A Call for Transparency and Accountability," May 2014. www.ftc.gov.
24. Quoted in Kroft, "The Data Brokers."
25. Quoted in Andrea Peterson, "These Data Brokers Cost Consumers Millions by Illegally Selling Off Their Financial Information, Says FTC," *Washington Post*, August 12, 2015. www.washingtonpost.com.

Chapter Two: Privacy and the Internet of Things

26. Keith Winstein, "Introducing the 'Right to Eavesdrop on Your Things,'" Politico, June 29, 2015. www.politico.com.
27. Winstein, "Introducing the 'Right to Eavesdrop on Your Things.'"
28. Winstein, "Introducing the 'Right to Eavesdrop on Your Things.'"
29. Quoted in Proofpoint Security, "Proofpoint Uncovers Internet of Things (IoT) Cyberattack," news release, January 16, 2014. http://investors.proofpoint.com.
30. Patrick Ziselberger, interview with author, March 17, 2016.
31. James Manyika, "What Is the Internet of Things Worth?," World Economic Forum, August 7, 2015. www.weforum.org.
32. Federal Bureau of Investigation, US Department of Transportation, and National Highway Traffic Safety Administration, "Motor Vehicles Increasingly Vulnerable to Remote Exploits," public service announcement, March 17, 2016. www.ic3.gov.
33. Federal Bureau of Investigation et al., "Motor Vehicles Increasingly Vulnerable to Remote Exploits."
34. Andy Greenberg, "Hackers Remotely Kill a Jeep on the Highway—with Me in It," *Wired*, July 21, 2015. www.wired.com.
35. Greenberg, "Hackers Remotely Kill a Jeep on the Highway—with Me in It."

36. Vivek Wadhwa, "Will the Coming 'Internet of Things' Mean the Death of Privacy?," *Huffington Post*, July 1, 2015. www.huffingtonpost.com.
37. Wadhwa, "Will the Coming 'Internet of Things' Mean the Death of Privacy?"
38. Wadhwa, "Will the Coming 'Internet of Things' Mean the Death of Privacy?"
39. Kashmir Hill, "When 'Smart Homes' Get Hacked: I Haunted a Complete Stranger's House via the Internet," *Forbes*, July 26, 2013. www.forbes.com.
40. *HIPAA Journal*, "New Information Released on Medical Informatics Engineering Data Breach," July 26, 2015. www.hipaajournal.com.
41. Quoted in Gina Kolata, "Web Hunt for DNA Sequences Leaves Privacy Compromised," *New York Times*, January 17, 2013. www.nytimes.com.
42. Federal Trade Commission, "FTC Report on Internet of Things Urges Companies to Adopt Best Practices to Address Consumer Privacy and Security Risks," news release, January 27, 2015. www.ftc.gov.
43. Justin Brookman, "Testimony of Justin Brookman Before Senate Commerce on Internet of Things," Center for Democracy & Technology, February 11, 2015. https://cdt.org.
44. Jacob Morgan, "A Simple Explanation of 'the Internet of Things,'" *Forbes*, May 13, 2014. www.forbes.com.

Chapter Three: Privacy, Security, and Social Media
45. Silverman, *Terms of Service*, p. viii.
46. Privacy Rights Clearinghouse, "Fact Sheet 35: Social Networking Privacy; How to Be Safe, Secure, and Social," February 2016. www.privacyrights.org.
47. Cooper Smith, "Social Big Data: The User Data Collected by Each of the World's Largest Social Networks—and What It Means," Business Insider, February 2, 2014. www.businessinsider.com.
48. Sarah Perez, "Twitter's New App Tracking Capabilities to Help Personalize User Experience, Benefit Advertisers," TechCrunch, November 26, 2014. http://techcrunch.com.
49. Kate Cox, "New Online Tool Shows You What the Heck Privacy Policies Actually Say," *Consumerist* (blog), March 11, 2016. https://consumerist.com.
50. Quoted in Brown, "How Can We Return Privacy Control to Social Media Users?"
51. Quoted in Cadie Thompson, "What You Really Sign Up For When You Use Social Media," CNBC, May 20, 2015. www.cnbc.com.
52. Theodore F. Claypoole, "Privacy and Social Media," *Business Law Today*, January 2014. www.americanbar.org.
53. Kim Komando, "Facebook Is Watching and Tracking You More than You Probably Realize," March 12, 2016. www.komando.com.

54. Paul Bischoff, "That 'Most Used Words' Facebook Quiz Is a Privacy Nightmare," Comparitech, November 22, 2015. www.comparitech.com.
55. Bischoff, "That 'Most Used Words' Facebook Quiz Is a Privacy Nightmare."
56. Komando, "Facebook Is Watching and Tracking You More than You Probably Realize."
57. Kim Komando, "Don't Click 'Like' on Facebook Again Until You Read This," February 27, 2016. www.komando.com.
58. Better Business Bureau, "Don't Fall for Fake Facebook Pages!," June 19, 2015. www.bbb.org.

Chapter Four: The Perils of Diminishing Online Privacy

59. Glenn Greenwald, "Why Privacy Matters," transcript, TED Talks, October 2014. www.ted.com.
60. Greenwald, "Why Privacy Matters."
61. Mike Godwin, "Our Inboxes, Ourselves," *Slate*, September 14, 2015. www.slate.com.
62. Daniel Solove, "Why Does Privacy Matter? One Scholar's Answer," *Atlantic*, February 26, 2014. www.theatlantic.com.
63. Solove, "Why Does Privacy Matter? One Scholar's Answer."
64. Brandon Griggs, "9 Ways Facebook Changed How We Talk," CNN, February 2, 2014. www.cnn.com.
65. Nancy Rothbard, "How to Save Your Career from Social Media Meltdown," *The Science of Work* (blog), *Psychology Today*, February 23, 2015. www.psychologytoday.com.
66. Rothbard, "How to Save Your Career from Social Media Meltdown."
67. Quoted in Alyssa Reyes, "Social Media Can Impact Future Employment," *California Aggie* (Davis, CA), February 14, 2014. https://theaggie.org.
68. Quoted in John Egan, "Oversharing on Social Media Can Cost You," Bankrate, 2016. www.bankrate.com.
69. Quoted in News Channel 10, "Findlay Waitress Fired for Facebook Post About Tipping," July 1, 2014. http://raycomgroup.worldnow.com.
70. Quoted in Beata Mostafavi, "'Sharenting' Trends: Do Parents Share Too Much About Their Kids on Social Media?," C.S. Mott Children's Hospital news release, March 16, 2015. www.mottchildren.org.
71. Quoted in Quentin Fottrell, "Read This Before Posting Photos of Your Kids on Facebook," MarketWatch, March 9, 2016. www.marketwatch.com.
72. Quoted in NYU Tandon School of Engineering, "A New Threat to Children's Online Privacy: Parents," May 12, 2015. http://engineering.nyu.edu.
73. Greenwald, "Why Privacy Matters."
74. Quoted in Tom Huddleston Jr., "Steve Wozniak: Edward Snowden Is a 'Hero to Me,'" *Fortune*, May 26, 2015. http://fortune.com.

75. Quoted in Spencer Ackerman and Sam Thielman, "US Intelligence Chief: We Might Use the Internet of Things to Spy on You," *Guardian* (Manchester), February 9, 2016. www.theguardian.com.
76. Trevor Timm, "The Government Just Admitted It Will Use Smart Home Devices for Spying," *Guardian* (Manchester), February 9, 2016. www.theguardian.com.
77. Anja Kaspersen, "Can You Have Both Security and Privacy in the Internet Age?," World Economic Forum, July 21, 2015. www.weforum.org.

Chapter Five: Protecting Online Privacy

78. Quoted in Kim Zetter, "California Now Has the Nation's Best Digital Privacy Law," *Wired*, October 8, 2015. www.wired.com.
79. Cory Doctorow, "Oakland Cops' License Cams Follow Drivers Everywhere," *Boing Boing* (blog), January 23, 2015. https://boingboing.net.
80. Matt Cagle, "Dirtbox over Disneyland? New Docs Reveal Anaheim's Cellular Surveillance Arsenal," American Civil Liberties Union, January 27, 2016. www.aclunc.org.
81. Quoted in Zetter, "California Now Has the Nation's Best Digital Privacy Law."
82. Cory Doctorow, "California Passes the Country's Best-Ever Privacy Law," *Boing Boing* (blog), October 9, 2015. http://boingboing.net.
83. Center for Democracy & Technology, "Electronic Communications Privacy Act Primer," May 13, 2015. https://cdt.org.
84. Center for Democracy & Technology, "Electronic Communications Privacy Act Primer."
85. Bob Goodlatte, "Chairman Goodlatte Opening Statement at Markup of H.R. 699, the 'Email Privacy Act,'" news release, April 13, 2016. https://judiciary.house.gov.
86. Quoted in Kevin Carty, "Senate Democrats Push for Security, Privacy Rules for Self-Driving Cars," Morning Consult, March 15, 2016. https://morningconsult.com.
87. Federal Trade Commission, "Internet of Things: Privacy & Security in a Connected World," FTC Staff Report, January 2015, pp. 28–29. www.ftc.gov.
88. Quoted in Federal Trade Commission, "FTC Report on Internet of Things Urges Companies to Adopt Best Practices to Address Consumer Privacy and Security Risks."
89. Rami Essaid, "Internet Privacy Is the Wrong Conversation," TechCrunch, April 26, 2015. http://techcrunch.com.
90. Essaid, "Internet Privacy Is the Wrong Conversation."
91. Aimee Picchi, "Why the Latest Hot Facebook App Is Raising Privacy Concerns," CBS News, November 25, 2015. www.cbsnews.com.
92. Quoted in Kristin Farley, "Expert Warns of the Dangers of 'Oversharing' on Social Media," WATE.com, January 19, 2016. http://wate.com.
93. David Cole, "Is Privacy Obsolete?," *Nation*, March 23, 2015. www.thenation.com.

ORGANIZATIONS TO CONTACT

American Civil Liberties Union (ACLU)
125 Broad St., 18th Floor
New York, NY 10004
phone: (212) 549-2500 • fax: (212) 549-2646
e-mail: aclu@aclu.org • website: www.aclu.org

The ACLU works with courts, legislatures, and communities to ensure that all individuals in the United States are afforded the rights and liberties guaranteed by the US Constitution. Hundreds of articles related to online privacy can be accessed through the organization's website.

Center for Democracy & Technology (CDT)
1401 K St. NW, Suite 200
Washington, DC 20005
phone: (202) 637-9800 • fax: (202) 637-0968
website: https://cdt.org

The CDT supports laws, corporate policies, and technology tools that protect the privacy of Internet users, and advocates for stronger legal controls on government surveillance. Its website offers press releases, news articles, information about online privacy campaigns, and a link to the CDT's blog.

Center for Digital Democracy
1621 Connecticut Ave., Suite 550
Washington, DC 20009
phone: (202) 986-2220
website: www.democraticmedia.org

The Center for Digital Democracy is a leading consumer protection and privacy organization that was founded in 2001. Its website offers press releases, information about its current projects, a special section on youth privacy and digital marketing, and a link to the *Need to Know* blog.

Electronic Frontier Foundation (EFF)
454 Shotwell St.
San Francisco, CA 94110-1914
phone: (415) 436-9333 • fax: (415) 436-9993
e-mail: information@eff.org • website: www.eff.org

The EFF is a civil liberties organization that advocates on behalf of the public interest with regard to issues such as free speech, privacy, innovation, and consumer rights. A vast amount of information about online privacy issues can be found on the EFF website, including white papers, press releases, news articles, legal cases, and a link to the EFF's blog.

Electronic Privacy Information Center (EPIC)
1718 Connecticut Ave. NW, Suite 200
Washington, DC 20009
phone: (202) 483-1140 • fax: (202) 483-1248
website: http://epic.org

EPIC is a public interest research center that seeks to focus public attention on civil liberties issues and to protect privacy, the First Amendment, and constitutional rights. Numerous reports, fact sheets, news articles, and videos related to online privacy issues can be accessed through the website.

Federal Communications Commission (FCC)
445 Twelfth St. SW
Washington, DC 20554
phone: (888) 225-5322 • fax: (866) 418-0232
website: www.fcc.gov

The FCC is an independent US government agency that regulates communications by radio, television, wire, satellite, and cable in all fifty states, the District of Columbia, and US territories. Numerous publications related to online privacy issues can be accessed through the website's search engine.

National Cyber Security Alliance
1010 Vermont Ave. NW
Washington, DC 20005
phone: (202) 525-5024
website: http://staysafeonline.org

Through education and awareness efforts, the National Cyber Security Alliance seeks to inform and empower individuals to use the Internet safely and securely. Numerous publications related to online privacy can be accessed through the website's search engine.

Patient Privacy Rights
1006 Mopac Circle, Suite 102
PO Box 248
Austin, TX 78767

phone: (512) 732-0033 • fax: (512) 732-0036
e-mail: privacy@patientprivacyrights.org
website: https://patientprivacyrights.org

Patient Privacy Rights is dedicated to protecting patient privacy by restoring people's control over their personal health information. Its website links to a variety of publications about patient privacy–related issues, and the search engine produces articles specifically about online privacy.

Privacy Rights Clearinghouse
3033 Fifth Ave., Suite 223
San Diego, CA 92103
phone: (619) 298-3396
website: www.privacyrights.org

The Privacy Rights Clearinghouse seeks to engage, educate, and empower people to be protective of their privacy. Its website offers fact sheets in English and Spanish, alerts about current online privacy issues, reports, and various other publications.

World Privacy Forum
3108 Fifth Ave., Suite B
San Diego, CA 92103
phone: (760) 712-4281
e-mail: info@worldprivacyforum.org
website: www.worldprivacyforum.org

Through independent privacy research, analysis, and consumer education, the World Privacy Forum seeks to empower people with the knowledge and tools they need to protect their online privacy. Its website offers reports, congressional testimonies, news releases, health privacy publications, and an alphabetized Key Issues section.

FOR FURTHER RESEARCH

Books

Julia Angwin, *Dragnet Nation: A Quest for Privacy, Security, and Freedom in a World of Relentless Surveillance*. New York: Times/Henry Holt, 2014.

Violet Blue, *The Smart Girl's Guide to Privacy: Practical Tips for Staying Safe Online*. San Francisco: No Starch, 2015.

Jon L. Mills, *Privacy in the New Media Age*. Gainesville: University Press of Florida, 2015.

Bruce Schneier, *Data and Goliath: The Hidden Battles to Collect Your Data and Control Your World*. New York: Norton, 2015.

Christine Wilcox, *Online Privacy*. San Diego: ReferencePoint, 2015.

David Haywood Young, *Take Back Your Privacy*. Seattle: CreateSpace, 2016.

Internet Sources

Cory Doctorow, "California Just Passed America's Best-Ever Online Privacy Law," *Boing Boing* (blog), October 9, 2015. http://boingboing.net/2015/10/09/california-passes-the-country.html.

Kim Komando, "Facebook Is Watching and Tracking You More than You Probably Realize," *USA Today*, March 18, 2016. www.usatoday.com/story/tech/columnist/komando/2016/03/18/facebook-watching-and-tracking-you-more-than-you-realize/81803796.

Gary Kovacs, "Why Online Privacy Matters," World Economic Forum, August 7, 2015. www.weforum.org/agenda/2015/08/why-online-privacy-matters.

Adrienne LaFrance, "How Self-Driving Cars Will Threaten Privacy," *Atlantic*, March 2016. www.theatlantic.com/technology/archive/2016/03/self-driving-cars-and-the-looming-privacy-apocalypse/474600.

Kevin Murnane, "How Men and Women Differ in Their Approach to Online Privacy and Security," *Forbes*, April 11, 2016. www.forbes.com/sites/kevinmurnane/2016/04/11/how-men-and-women-differ-in-their-approach-to-online-privacy-and-security/#34d52c5018b0.

Rawn Shah, "Do Privacy Concerns Really Change with the Internet of Things?," *Forbes*, July 2, 2015. www.forbes.com/sites/rawnshah/2015/07/02/do-privacy-concerns-really-change-with-the-internet-of-things/#7f9fd37640bc.

Tom Wheeler, "It's Your Data: Empowering Consumers to Protect Online Privacy," *Huffington Post*, March 10, 2016. www.huffingtonpost.com/tom-wheeler/its-your-data-protect-online-privacy_b_9428484.html.

Websites

ConnectSafely (www.connectsafely.org). ConnectSafely is an interactive online-only resource for parents, teens, educators, and others who are interested in learning more about Internet safety, security, and privacy.

NSTeens.org (www.nsteens.org). NSTeens.org is designed to help teach young people about the importance of making safer choices while on the Internet. The site offers videos, games, comics, and quizzes.

SafeTeens.com (www.safeteens.com). This site provides information about staying safe online. It features articles about protecting privacy and links to other online safety resources for young people.

INDEX

Note: Boldface page numbers indicate illustrations.

AboutTheData.com, 54
Accenture, 31
Acxiom, 14, 18, 54
advertising
   pre-Internet information gathering for, 9
   self-driving cars and, 24
   targeted
      data brokers and, 18
      data mining for, 9
      social media and hyper-, 33
      value of, 36–37
Alabama, 62
American Action Forum, 28
American Recovery and Reinvestment Act (2009), 28
Anderson, Joel, 57
Angwin, Julia, 8, 17–18
Annenberg School for Communication (University of Pennsylvania), 6–7
App Graph, 34
apps
   collection of data by third-party, 38–39
   mobile, 15, 33–34
Atlantic (magazine), 24

baby role-playing community on Instagram, 49
Bartlett, Jamie, 61
behavioral advertising. *See* targeted advertising
Better Business Bureau, 41
Bischoff, Paul, 39
Bitglass Healthcare Breach Report, 28
Blumenthal, Richard, 59–60
BMW AG, 23
Brill, Julie, 14
Brookman, Justin, 30–31
Brown, Jerry, 56, **59**
browser histories, 12
Burger King lettuce incident, 11
Business Insider, 33

Cagle, Matt, 57
California Electronic Communications Privacy Act (CalECPA, 2015), 56–57
canvas fingerprinting, 12–13

Center for Democracy & Technology (CDT), 58
Chevrolet Volt, 23
children, unauthorized use of pictures of, 49, 50–51
Clapper, James, 52–53
Clark, Sarah J., 50
Claypoole, Theodore F., 36
Cleveland Scene (newspaper), 11
Cole, David, 66
consumer information
   inaccurate, 37, 54
   sources of
      cookies, 9–12, 41
      digital fingerprinting, 12–13
      exchangeable image file (EXIF) data, 11
      mobile apps, 15, 33–34
      supercookies, 12
      See also social media, as sources of information
consumers
   believe already have lost control over privacy, 7
   consider data collection fair, 6
   do not consider data collection fair, 6–7
   lack of awareness of extent of personal information known, 14–15
   supposed lack of concern about invasions of privacy, 44–45
   typical digital broker categories, 17
Cook, Timothy D., 4, 5
cookies, 9–12, 41
Cox, Kate, 34

data breaches, 7, 28
data brokers
   anonymized data, 18, 29, 30
   customers of, 14, 18
   estimated number of, 14
   examples of, 14, 17, 18, 54
   profiling categories, 15–17
   purpose of, 13
   sources of information, 14
data collection. *See* data mining
data mining
   consumers consider, fair, 6
   consumers do not consider, fair, 6–7
   described, 4–5

for targeted advertising, 9
    See also data brokers
Dean, Bill, 66
Delphi Automotive, 60
digital bread crumbs
    described, 9
    See also consumer information; social media, as sources of information
digital cameras, EXIF data captured by, 11
digital fingerprinting, 12–13
digital profiles, 17
dirtboxes, 57
Doctorow, Cory, 57, 58
dossiers, 17
Dragnet Nation (Angwin), 8
Dropcam, 53

Electronic Communications Privacy Act (1986), 45–46, 58, 59
electronic control units (ECUs), 23
Electronic Frontier Foundation, 56
electronic health records (EHRs), 28–30
Email Privacy Act (H.R. 699, proposed 2016), 58–59
employment and social media monitoring, 48–49
Essaid, Rami, 62–63
exchangeable image file (EXIF) data, 11

Facebook, **6**
    as customer of data brokers, 18
    data collected by, 33
    European investigation of, 41–43
    on extensiveness of data collection practices, 5
    "liking" and like farming, 40–41, **41**, 43
    logging on to other sites through, 41–42
    Partner Categories for tailoring advertisements, 18
    privacy statement, 34, **38**
    third-party apps integrate with, 38
    type of data saved, 8
Federal Trade Commission (FTC)
    data brokers and
        awareness of, 14
        characteristics of targets of, 17
        complaints filed against, 18–19
    number of connected devices in use worldwide, 30
    recommended measures to safeguard privacy in Internet of Things, 60–62
Five W's of tracking, 63
Forbes (magazine), 31
Fourth Amendment (US Constitution), 45, 58, 59

"free" services, 5
free thought and speech, privacy as safeguard for, 46

games online, 38–39
General Motors (GM), 23, 54, 60
Gen X Marketing Group, 19
geolocation information in EXIF data, 11
GMR Transcription Services, 60–61
Godwin, Mike, 45
Goodlatte, Bob, 59
Google
    Dropcam, 53
    reads personal e-mail, 26
    saves all web searches, 8
    tracking of YouTube watching, 26
government surveillance
    federal protections are outdated, 45–46, 58, 59
    retention of rights underpinning democracy and, 55
    by smart devices, 52–53
    Snowden revelations, 52
    stingrays for, 57
GPS tracking, 56
Gralla, Preston, 29
Greenberg, Andy, 25–26
Greenwald, Glenn, 44–45, 52
Griggs, Brandon, 46

hacking
    fears of millennials, 37
    of medical records, 28
    smart cars, 23–26
    vulnerability of Internet of Things, 21–22, **22**, 27
health information
    profiling according to, 15–17, **16**
    records
        data mining of, 29–30
        hacking of electronic, 28
        state protections, 62
        stored unencrypted, 60–61
Hill, Kashmir, 27
HIPAA Journal, 28
Holland, Marcie Kirk, 48

Ideal Financial Solutions, 19
Illinois, 62
information brokers. *See* data brokers
InfoUSA, 17
Instagram, **35**, 49
Internet of Things
    ability to collect data by listening to conversations, 21–22, 24, 53–54

complexity of connecting, 29
described, 20
growth of, 31
learning algorithms, 21–22
positive aspects of connectivity, 30
privacy safeguards recommended by FTC, 60–62
smartphones connected to, **22**
surveillance by US government and, 52–53
use by law enforcement, 53
vulnerability to hacking, 21–22, **22**, 27
Internet protocol (IP) address, described, 10

Jeep Cherokee, 25–26
Jia, Haiyan, 42

Kamkar, Samy, 23
Kaspersen, Anja, 55
Komando, Kim, 38, 39, 40
Kovacs, Gary, 15
Kuznetsov, Eugene, 12

LaFrance, Adrienne, 24
law enforcement
  search warrants
    proposed federal law, 58–59
    state laws, 56–57
  use of Internet of Things, 53
  use of license cams and stingrays, 57
learning algorithms, 21–22
Leno, Mark, 57
license cams, 57
like farming, 40–41, 43

Manyika, James, 22
Markey, Ed, 59–60
Mayer, Jonathan, 54
McGuire, Amy L., 30
Medical Informatics Engineering, 28
medical information
  profiling according to, 15–17, **16**
  records
    data mining of, 29–30
    hacking of electronic, 28
    state protections, 62
    stored unencrypted, 60–61
Meulen, Brenda Vander, 48
Miller, Charlie, 25–26
Minkus, Tehila, 51
mobile apps, 15, 33–34
Morgan, Jacob, 31
Most Used Words on Facebook (app), 39

National Highway Traffic Safety Administration (NHTSA)

cybersecurity issues in smart cars, 24–25
electronic control units in smart cars and, 23
proposed mandatory cybersecurity and privacy standards, 59–60
National Security Agency (NSA), 52
"Nation Under A-Hack" (USA Network), 37
New Mexico, 62
New York University, 51
NYU Shanghai, 51

1000 Genomes Project, 30
Osterman, Michael, 21
oversharing, 47–51, 66
Ozer, Nicole, 56

Panda Security, 10–11
Paramount Lists, 17
Penn State University, 42
Perez, Sarah, 34
permacookies, 12
personal information, defining, 62
Personal Information Protection Act (Illinois), 62
Pew Research Center, 15, 35, 39
Picchi, Aimee, 64–66
Polytechnic School of Engineering (New York University), 51
privacy
  constitutional right to, 4, 45
  federal protections are outdated, 45–46, 58
  as limit to government power, 46
  as safeguard for freedom of thought and speech, 46
  state protections, 56–57, 62
  vulnerability of, 66
Privacy Rights Clearinghouse, 12–13, 32
profiling, 15–17, **16**
Proofpoint, 21
ProPublica, 13

quizzes online, 38–39

Ramirez, Edith, 9, 13, 62
Rauner, Bruce, 62
Reitman, Rainey, 7
Response Solutions, 17
Rich, Jessica, 19
Rothbard, Nancy, 47–48

Samsung Smart TVs, 53
search warrants
  proposed federal law, 58–59
  state laws, 56–57
  US Constitution and, 58

security issues, consumer notification of, 62
security patches, 20–21
self-censorship, 65
self-driving cars, 24, 60, **63**
Sell, Nico, 35–36, 65
Sequoia One LLC, 19
sharing, 46–47, 49–51
Sherbit, 17, 18
Silverman, Jacob
   on extensiveness of Facebook's data collection practices, 5
   on privacy statements, 35
   on social media activity, 32
   on ultimate receivers of consumer information, 14
smart cars, 23–26
smart devices, ability to collect data by listening to conversations, 21–22, 24, 53–54
Smart Insights, 32
smartphones
   apps, 15, 33–34
   Internet of Things connection to, **22**
   measures to protect privacy, 65–66
   surveillance of, using stingrays, 57
Smith, Cooper, 33
Snowden, Edward, 52, **53**
social media
   attitude of millennials toward, 37
   average daily use of, 33
   employment and monitoring of, 48–49
   measures to enhance security of, 64–66
   number of users worldwide, 32
   privacy statements, 34–36
   as sources of information, **13**, 14
      oversharing on, 47–48, 51, 66
      ownership and sale of personal data posted on, 36–37
      public nature of all actions and data on, 47
      sharing on, 46–47, 49–51
      third-party apps and, 38–39
      use by teenagers, 42
      See also specific websites such as Facebook
Solove, Daniel, 46
South Dakota, 62
Sparapani, Tim, 14–15, 17
Statlistics, 17
stingrays, 57
Stockley, Mark, 10
supercookies, 12

Tanner, Adam, 16–17
targeted advertising

data brokers and, 18
data mining for, 9
social media and hyper-, 33
value of, 36–37
Taylor, Harriet, 65
TechCrunch, 34
teenagers, use of social media by, 42
Terms of Service: Social Media and the Price of Constant Connection (Silverman), 5, 32
Tor, 61
tracking
   disclosure by sites of what data is collected and shared, 63
   Five W's, 63
   by Google, 26
   measures users should take to enhance security, 64–66
   methods used
      cookies, 9–12, 41
      digital fingerprinting, 12–13
      exchangeable image file (EXIF) data, 11
      mobile apps, 15, 33–34
      supercookies, 12
   See also social media, as sources of information
transparency, importance of, 62–63
Trimm, Trevor, 54–55
Turow, Joseph, 6–7
Twitter, 33–34, 64

Uhls, Yalda T., 51
University of Pennsylvania, 6–7
USA Network, 37
US Constitution, 45, 59
   privacy, as fundamental right, 4
   warrant requirement, 58
US government, surveillance by, 52–53

Valasek, Chris, 25–26
"virtual spies," 10–11
voice command issues, 21–22
Vonvon, 39

Wadhwa, Vivek, 26–27
Warner, Timothy L., 11
web searches, Google saving of, 8
Winstein, Keith, 20–21
World Privacy Forum, 14
Wozniak, Steve, 52

YouTube, 26

Zaneis, Mike, 6
Ziselberger, Patrick, 21–22
zombie cookies, 12